The Harcourt Brace Casebook Series in Literature

"A Good Man Is Hard to Find"

Flannery O'Connor

THE HARCOURT BRACE CASEBOOK SERIES IN LITERATURE
Series Editors: Laurie G. Kirszner and Stephen R. Mandell

DRAMA
Athol Fugard
"Master Harold" . . . and the boys

William Shakespeare
Hamlet

POETRY
Emily Dickinson
A Collection of Poems

Langston Hughes
A Collection of Poems

FICTION
Charlotte Perkins Gilman
"The Yellow Wallpaper"

Flannery O'Connor
"A Good Man Is Hard to Find"

John Updike
"A&P"

Eudora Welty
"A Worn Path"

The Harcourt Brace Casebook Series in Literature
Series Editors: Laurie G. Kirszner and Stephen R. Mandell

"A Good Man Is Hard to Find"

Flannery O'Connor

Contributing Editor

Laura Mandell Zaidman
University of South Carolina Sumter

Harcourt College Publishers

Fort Worth   Philadelphia   San Diego   New York   Orlando   Austin   San Antonio
Toronto   Montreal   London   Sydney   Tokyo

Publisher	Earl McPeek
Acquisitions Editor	Claire Brantley
Developmental Editor	Jana Pitts
Project Editor	Claudia Gravier
Art Director	Garry Harman
Production Manager	James McDonald

ISBN: 0-15-507470-9
Library of Congress Catalog Card Number: 99-62186

Address for Domestic Orders
Harcourt College Publishers, 6277 Sea Harbor Drive, Orlando, FL 32887-6777
800-782-4479

Address for International Orders
International Customer Service
Harcourt Inc., 6277 Sea Harbor Drive, Orlando, FL 32887-6777
407-345-3800
(fax) 407-345-4060
(e-mail) hbintl@harcourtbrace.com

Address for Editorial Correspondence
Harcourt College Publishers, 301 Commerce Street, Suite 3700, Fort Worth, TX 76102

Web Site Address
http://www.harcourtcollege.com

Harcourt College Publishers will provide complimentary supplements or supplement packages to those adopters qualified under our adoption policy. Please contact your sales representative to learn how you qualify. If as an adopter or potential user you receive supplements you do not need, please return them to your sales representative or send them to: Attn: Returns Department, Troy Warehouse, 465 South Lincoln Drive, Troy, MO 63379.

Printed in the United States of America

9 0 1 2 3 4 5 6 7 8 066 9 8 7 6 5 4 3 2 1

Harcourt College Publishers

ABOUT THE SERIES

The Harcourt Brace Casebook Series in Literature has its origins in our anthology *Literature: Reading, Reacting, Writing* (third edition, 1997), which in turn arose out of our many years of teaching college writing and literature courses. The primary purpose of each casebook in the series is to offer students a convenient, self-contained reference tool that they can use to complete a research project for an introductory literature course.

In choosing subjects for the casebooks, we draw on our own experience in the classroom, selecting works of poetry, fiction, and drama that students like to read, discuss, and write about and that teachers like to teach. Unlike other collections of literary criticism aimed at student audiences, the Harcourt Brace Casebook Series in Literature features short stories, groups of poems, or plays (rather than longer works, such as novels) because these are the genres most often taught in college-level introduction to Literature courses. In selecting particular authors and titles, we focus on those most popular with students and those most accessible to them.

To facilitate student research—and to facilitate instructor supervision of that research—each casebook contains all the resources students need to produce a documented research paper on a particular work of literature. Every casebook in the series includes the following elements:

- A comprehensive **introduction** to the work, providing social, historical, and political background. This introduction helps students to understand the work and the author in context of a particular time and place. In particular, the introduction enables students to appreciate customs, situations, and events that may have contributed to the author's choice of subject matter, emphasis, or style.

- A **headnote,** including birth and death dates of the author; details of the work's first publication and its subsequent publication history, if relevant; details about the author's life; a summary of the author's career; and a list of key published works, with dates of publication.

- The most widely accepted version of the **literary work,** along with the explanatory footnotes students will need to understand unfamiliar terms and concepts or references to people, places, or events.

- **Discussion questions** focusing on themes developed in the work. These questions, designed to stimulate critical thinking and discussion, can also serve as springboards for research projects.

- Several extended **research assignments** related to the literary work. Students may use these assignments exactly as they appear in the casebook, or students or instructors may modify the assignments to suit their own needs or research interests.

- A diverse collection of traditional and non-traditional **secondary sources,** which may include scholarly articles, reviews, interviews, memoirs, newspaper articles, historical documents, and so on. This resource offers students access to sources they might not turn to on their own—for example, a popular song that inspired a short story, a story that was the original version of a play, a legal document that sheds light on a work's theme, or two different biographies of an author—thus encouraging students to look beyond the obvious or the familiar as they search for ideas. Students may use only these sources, or they may supplement them with sources listed in the casebook's bibliography (see below).

- An annotated model **student research paper** drawing on several of the casebook's secondary sources. This paper uses MLA parenthetical documentation and includes a Works Cited list conforming to MLA style.

- A comprehensive **bibliography** of print and electronic sources related to the work. This bibliography offers students an opportunity to move beyond the sources in the casebook to other sources related to a particular research topic.

- A concise **guide to MLA documentation,** including information on what kinds of information require documentation (and what kinds do not); a full explanation of how to construct parenthetical references and how to place them in a paper; sample parenthetical reference format for various kinds of sources used in papers about literature; a complete explanation of how to assemble a list of Works Cited, accompanied by sample works cited entries (including formats for documenting electronic sources); and guidelines for using explanatory notes (with examples).

By collecting all this essential information in one convenient place, each volume in the Harcourt Brace casebook Series in Literature responds to the needs of both students and teachers. For students, the casebooks offer convenience, referentiality, and portability that make the process of doing research easier. Thus, the casebooks recognize what students already know: that Introduction to Literature is not their only class and that the literature research paper is not their only assignment. For instructors, the casebooks offer a rare combination of flexibility and control in the classroom. For example, teachers may choose to assign one casebook or more than one; thus, they have the option of having all students in a class write about the same work or having different groups of students, or individual students to use only the secondary sources collected in the casebook, thereby controlling students' use of (and acknowledgment of) sources more closely, or they may encourage students to seek both print and electronic sources beyond those included in the casebook. By building convenience, structure, and flexibility into each volume, we have designed The Harcourt Brace casebook Series in Literature to suit a wide variety of teaching styles and research interests. The casebooks have made the research paper an easier project for us and a less stressful one for our students; we hope they will do the same for you.

Laurie G. Kirszner
Stephen R. Mandell
Series Editors

PREFACE

Flannery O'Connor published "A Good Man Is Hard to Find" in the anthology *The Avon Book of Modern Writing* (1953) and then revised it as the title story for her 1955 collection, *A Good Man Is Hard to Find and Other Stories.* This popular, widely anthologized story has attracted much critical attention with its startling use of violence. "A Good Man Is Hard to Find" forces readers to reflect on religious questions of God's grace and judgment while at the same time balancing comedy and tragedy. This story, with its full range of human emotions and theological issues, was O'Connor's favorite to read to college audiences.

O'Connor continually revised her writing. As she explained to an Atlanta journalist, "I write every day. But often nothing comes of my efforts. They don't lead anywhere. I rewrite, edit, throw away. It's slow and searching" (Magee 91). Consequently, her work provides an excellent example for students engaged in the writing process for composition and literature courses. For instance, the story's earlier version has the family taking a detour onto a dirt road because of road construction. By revising the plot to make the detour the grandmother's idea, O'Connor makes her responsible for the consequences of her actions. But who is ultimately responsible for the tragic murders? Is The Misfit guiltier than the grandmother? Critics have focused on the dynamics of the encounter between these two characters to determine the story's overall meaning.

This casebook contains secondary sources that provide analysis and commentary on "A Good Man Is Hard to Find." In addition, some of O'Connor's letters and essays, scholars' criticism, and a student's research paper offer different perspectives for analyzing and writing about the story. These selections represent a variety of accessible critical sources; also, you can research beyond this casebook by exploring the primary and secondary sources in the bibliography. Although a few critics fault the story's structure, tone, and point of view, most scholars consider "A Good Man Is Hard to Find" a well-crafted work. As the bibliography shows, O'Connor scholarship is extensive and varied. The secondary sources collected in this casebook reflect an assortment of approaches to literary criticism.

- Asals, Frederick. "The Aesthetics of Incongruity" (1982). In this chapter from *Flannery O'Connor: The Imagination of Extremity*, Asals analyzes the themes and methods that make "A Good Man Is Hard to Find" O'Connor's best-known work.

- Bellamy, Michael O. "Everything Off Balance: Protestant Election in Flannery O'Connor's 'A Good Man Is Hard to Find'" (1979). Bellamy shows how O'Connor illustrates the Protestant doctrine of election with the grandmother's conversion, which comes suddenly after a climactic moment of grace. He also quotes O'Connor's statement that "all good stories are about conversion."

- Bryant, Hallman B. "Reading the Map in 'A Good Man Is Hard to Find'" (1981). Why is Timothy the only fictional location in the story? Bryant argues that O'Connor alludes to I Timothy in the New Testament— Paul's pastoral letter admonishing people to lead a righteous life—as a way to show the faults of the grandmother's family.

- Butler, Rebecca R. "What's So Funny About Flannery O'Connor?" (1980). Butler approaches O'Connor's work from the American comic tradition by pointing out the humor in titles, names of characters, places, and dialogue. She suggests that O'Connor's uses violence to heighten the comedy and to avoid sentimentality.

- Coulthard, A. R. "Flannery O'Connor's Deadly Conversions" (1984). Coulthard asserts that O'Connor serves both her God and her muse by presenting the grandmother's redemption at the time of her death.

- Green, Eddie. "A Good Man Is Hard to Find" (1917). This famous blues song was written by Eddie Green and made popular by Bessie Smith, as well as other singers.

- Highsmith, Dixie Lee. "Flannery O'Connor's Polite Conversation" (1982). Highsmith analyzes the language interaction between characters to show how O'Connor's use of clichés enriches the story's theme. These popular sayings take on added meaning and provide insights into life's mysteries.

- Jones, Madison. "A Good Man's Predicament" (1984). Jones presents both O'Connor's and his own explanation of The Misfit's sudden violence. Seen together, these two interpretations give O'Connor's story added dimension.

- O'Connor, Flannery. Letter from *The Habit of Being: Letters of Flannery O'Connor* (1961, 1979). Ed. Sally Fitzgerald. In a letter to a college English professor, O'Connor corrects the faulty interpretation of "A Good Man Is Hard to Find" by a group of university students and professors.

- ---. "On Her Own Work" from *Mystery and Manners: Occasional Prose* (1963, 1969). Ed. Sally and Robert Fitzgerald. O'Connor gives her interpretation of "A Good Man Is Hard to Find" to a Hollins College (Roanoke, Virginia) audience.

- Tate, J. O., Jr. "A Good Source Is Not So Hard to Find" (1980). Tate's research from several 1952 newspaper articles provides insight into the naming of The Misfit and the development of his characterization.

- Walker, Alice. "Beyond the Peacock: The Reconstruction of Flannery O'Connor" (1984). Walker recounts a trip with her mother to their former house and to O'Connor's farmhouse not far away. Besides describing the farm's majestic peacocks and praising the writer's genius, Walker discusses O'Connor's black characters.

Following O'Connor's story and the secondary sources, you will find discussion questions and research topics to help you in thinking and writing about your own interpretations. Then, Renae Martin, a University of South Carolina Sumter student, provides an essay to illustrate the proper use of MLA style to document sources from this casebook. In writing about "A Good Man Is Hard to Find," Renae combines her own ideas with critics' views as she examines the story's main characters and dominant theme. This casebook also includes a bibliography of relevant print and electronic sources, as well as a section on documentation.

Acknowledgments

I am grateful to the many people who made this casebook a reality, especially the English editorial staff at Harcourt Brace: Camille Adkins, developmental editor; Claire Brantley, acquisitions editor; Jana Pitts, developmental editor; Claudia Gravier, project editor; James McDonald, production manager; Garry Harman, art director; and Mary Sanders, copyeditor. I sincerely thank Laurie G. Kirszner and Stephen R. Mandell, the casebook series editors, who have allowed me to write about my favorite

Flannery O'Connor story. I am indebted to Sarah Gordon, distinguished editor of the *Flannery O'Connor Bulletin,* who generously reviewed this manuscript and offered many valuable suggestions. In 1978 the *Flannery O'Connor Bulletin* published my first article, so over two decades later, my work on O'Connor has come full circle. Sally Fitzgerald inspired me when we met in Macon, Georgia, in 1980 and traveled to Milledgeville together. I especially appreciate the loving support of my family: Deborah Zaidman; Barry, Marilyn, and Keren Mandell; Cindy and Adam Lourie; Rachel, Don, Alexa, and Emma Van Demark, and the Kenners. I am fortunate to have the institutional support of the University of South Carolina Sumter, and to be blessed with good friends: Patricia Alt, Paula Feldman, Cara-lin Getty, Lois Gibson, Susan Goldstein, David Grossman, Hayes Hampton, Betty Harvey, Susan Hendley, Caroline Hunt, Michael Joseph, Meena Khorana, Rodney Lawrence, Revelle Magidovitch, Renae Martin, Jerry Naylor, Tom Powers, Eric Reisenauer, Sandy Richardson, John Safford, and Jane Luther Smith. Good people *are* hard to find, but once found, they certainly enrich the enjoyment of life.

Laura Mandell Zaidman
Sumter, South Carolina
June 1999

CONTENTS

Sample Student Research Paper 109

Bibliography 121

Appendix: Documenting Sources 133

Credits 147

Introduction

The World of
Flannery O'Connor

"I sold 'A Good Man Is Hard to Find' to the *Partisan Review Reader,* another of those 50¢ jobs," wrote Flannery O'Connor on June 7, 1953, to her friends Sally and Robert Fitzgerald (Fitzgerald, *HB* 59). O'Connor neither struck it rich from her writing nor published a large number of books. In her lifetime, only two novels and two short story collections appeared; then after she died in 1964, her collected stories, essays, book reviews, and letters were published. Sally Fitzgerald edited *The Habit of Being: Letters of Flannery O'Connor* (1979), which details O'Connor's career and private life—especially the joy she found in her family and friendships. These remarkable letters paint portraits of her and her world.

The absurdities and quirks of human nature provided O'Connor with amusing anecdotes for her letters. As Fitzgerald relates, O'Connor delighted her friends with funny advertisements for products or for a gospel quartet. She found hilarious birth announcements for babies with unbelievable names and gleefully passed along bizarre news items, such as the attendance of Roy Rogers's horse at a California church service. Another example of human perversity which caught her eye is the newspaper photo with a caption about a child of seven, adorned with crimped hair and ribbons, who won an amateur talent contest by singing the blues song 'A Good Man Is Hard to Find'" (Fitzgerald, *HB* xi). When telling these stories in her letters, O'Connor wrote in a down-home, Southern dialect marked by ungrammatical constructions and creative spelling. However, when discussing literary or theological matters, she shifted to a serious, educated style of writing. Her letters, interviews, and essays vividly describe her world—her personal life and writing career, along with some of the social, cultural, historical, and political context for "A Good Man Is Hard to Find."

2

AFTER WORLD WAR II

O'Connor's characters reflect the larger perspective of a violent world torn asunder by war—especially the horrific genocide of Europe's Jews by the Nazis. By understanding that the "real world" intersects with the fictional world, the reader gains further insights into "A Good Man Is Hard to Find." In the story, Red Sammy Butts (owner of The Tower restaurant) is a veteran dressed in khaki trousers, probably government-issued. He discusses the pitiful world situation with the grandmother, who says that "Europe was entirely to blame for the way things were now" and "the way Europe acted you would think we were made of money. . . ." (O'Connor, 25). Their conversation mimics the babbling at the Tower of Babel in the Bible. If the grandmother had her way, the United States would never have rescued Western Europe from the aftermath of war and the Holocaust.

Because O'Connor employs violence for dramatic emphasis, the reader can better grasp the story's themes by understanding the story's historical, political, and economic setting. World War II left millions dead in battle and in concentration camps. People worldwide desperately needed to find the good in humanity. In 1947 Winston Churchill called Western Europe "a rubble heap, a charnel house, a breeding ground for pestilence and hate" (Blum et al. 768). The dramatic recovery of war-torn economies across Western Europe, aided by the Marshall Plan, reduced the political threat of Communism and allowed the region to assume independence in the world community in the 1950s. Americans offered additional assistance to Europe's refugees by allowing them to immigrate to the United States and by supporting the creation of Israel.

After World War II, the world entered the Cold War, and the peacetime, for which it had so dearly paid, vanished. This Cold War began when Soviet Communism threatened Europe. The antagonism between the United States and the Soviet Union escalated with the Soviets' expansion across Europe. Americans faced the possibility that Joseph Stalin's Russia might succeed in conquering Europe, the same goal Hitler had attempted. Even without direct Russian military action, compliant Communist parties gained control in several countries. To stop further Russian expansion, the United States took political and economic action. Once the Communist threat seemed contained, leaders decided against military action to overthrow the Soviet regimes. At the time, the United States did not seem overly alarmed once Communism's spread appeared to be halted; for instance, in 1948 President Harry S. Truman even referred to Joseph Stalin as "Uncle Joe." This feeling of family unity did not last long, however.

The witch-hunt for Communists had begun by 1949 and, in fact, controversy raged at Yaddo, the artists' colony in Saratoga Springs, New York where O'Connor worked on her first novel (1948–49). O'Connor comments about the American Communist Party in one published letter (see Fitzgerald, *HB* 11–12). Her characters, in addition, sometimes reflect the paranoia fueled by Cold War hostilities. For example, Red Sammy—who advertises on one sign, "A VETERAN!"—repeats his anguish about the sad state of the world, saying, "You can't win . . . These days you don't know who to trust" (O'Connor, 25). Another O'Connor story, "A Circle in the Fire," has been interpreted as a commentary on Americans' fear of a Soviet invasion. By the end of the 1940s, Americans had committed themselves to fighting communism. The Truman Doctrine was the result, promising to guard world freedom.

The Soviet Union responded to the Truman Doctrine by consolidating control of Eastern Europe and dominating its satellites. Stalin eradicated political dissent as the West watched helplessly. However, when the Soviet Union blockaded West Berlin's highway, river, and rail traffic, the Western powers supplied food and other necessities to the isolated West Berliners through a successful airlift and established a counter-blockade of East Germany. On May 12, 1949, the Soviet blockade ended. In October 1950, United Nations forces crossed the 38th parallel between Communist North Korea and U.S.-backed South Korea. By the time the Korean War ended in July 1953, more than 33,000 Americans had died in battle. The Cold War's clash of interests and ideologies intensified throughout the 1950s.

POLITICAL BATTLES ON THE HOME FRONT

In addition to dealing with international Cold War hostilities, President Truman had to convert a war economy to a peacetime one. Within a year after his election, phrases such as "To err is Truman" entered the political language, and Republicans won the majority of Congressional seats in the midterm election. However, in 1948 Truman ran against New York Governor Thomas E. Dewey. Truman waged a cross-country "give-'em-hell" campaign lambasting the record of the "do-nothing, good-for-nothing" Republican Congress. The public-opinion polls forecast a resounding Republican victory (and the *Chicago Tribune* even prematurely announced Dewey the winner), but Truman beat Dewey in the popular vote by two million. A famous photograph shows a grinning, newly elected Truman holding up the newspaper with the headline proclaiming "Dewey Defeats Truman."

The extremely close presidential election showed a divided nation—especially a South different from the rest of the country. South Carolina's

States' Rights Dixiecrat Strom Thurmond carried four Southern states with more than one million votes. Another Southerner, Henry A. Wallace, who headed the liberal Progressive Party, also garnered more than one million votes. On the other hand, the South still had loyal liberal Democrats, black and white, who had supported Franklin Delano Roosevelt in the 1930s and early 1940s.

More divisiveness came when Wisconsin Senator Joseph R. McCarthy conducted his infamous "witch-hunt" for Communists through hearings by the House Un-American Activities Committee. Infuriated by McCarthy's blatant abuse of political power, Truman denounced McCarthy for threatening the freedom of every American. McCarthy's destructive investigation, however, dominated media coverage for four years before the Senate finally censured him for unethical behavior.

In the 1952 presidential election campaign, the war against alleged Communist sympathizers came to the forefront as Dwight D. Eisenhower, with his running mate Richard M. Nixon, challenged Adlai E. Stevenson. Governor Stevenson of Illinois, a brilliant scholar and eloquent speaker, had been relatively unknown nationally. Detractors mocked him and his intellectual supporters as "eggheads." During this bitter campaign, Republicans denounced the Democrats' legacy of the Korean War, the spread of Communism, and corruption in government. Nixon lambasted his opponent as "Adlai the appeaser." Having played an important role in exposing former State Department official Alger Hiss as a Communist spy and having him convicted for perjury in 1950, Nixon now accused the Democrats of being cowardly in supporting Communist containment and in covering up the alleged "Communist conspiracy." During his campaign, Eisenhower refused to confront McCarthy, even when the Senator personally accused Eisenhower's friends of being involved in the supposed Communist plot to overthrow the government.

O'Connor, fascinated with this heated campaign, wrote to the Fitzgeralds in the summer of 1952: "Much politicking around here. The lady across the street went down and got herself an Eisenhower button the other day and that afternoon he said he would put a qualified Negro in the cabinet if he could find one. She returned the button before that evening sun went down. Maw is for Eisenhower but Stevenson is good enough for me though I hope he has quit applying the words of Christ to himself" (Fitzgerald, *HB* 42).

General Eisenhower won decisively. But he did not put a "qualified Negro" in his cabinet; nor did he act soon enough to challenge McCarthy's reckless destruction of people's reputations and careers. He initially retreated from any confrontation by explaining that he would not "get in the gutter with that guy" (Blum et al. 792). However, to quell widespread panic about Communists in government and other powerful places, the President finally spoke out in June 1953 against the banning, and even burning, of books about Communist ideology. McCarthy finally lost support when the Senate denounced him in televised hearings in 1954 after he falsely accused the U.S. Army of harboring Communist spies.

Eisenhower took office in 1953, the year "A Good Man Is Hard to Find" first appeared in print. Americans saw him as a good man—one who could end the Korean War and rampant McCarthyism. He had emerged a hero from World War II as Supreme Commander of the Allied Forces in Europe. Then he served as head of NATO and as president of Columbia University. People hoped he would heal America's wounds caused by violence and factionalism, and restore peace (Blum et al. 788). Eisenhower's conservative administration came closer to meeting the expectations of U.S. business and industry. In fact, Secretary of Defense Charles E. Wilson (a former General Motors executive) announced that he saw no conflict between his business and political commitments because "what was good for our country was good for General Motors, and *vice versa*" (Blum et al. 790).

BATTLE FOR CIVIL RIGHTS

In 1947 Truman's Committee on Civil Rights had recommended the elimination of segregation based on race, color, creed, or national origin. The Committee attacked the "separate but equal" doctrine (which stemmed from the 1896 Supreme Court case of *Plessy v. Ferguson*), calling it inconsistent with the basic egalitarianism of the American way of life. This Committee also advocated a federal act to prohibit employment discrimination; it proposed withholding federal funds from segregated schools, public housing, and public health facilities. Although Truman ended segregation in the military, he failed to convince Congress to pass his civil rights program.

In the 1950s, civil rights leaders increased their demands for equality and freedom. Most notable of the legal battles won are those of lawyer Thurgood Marshall (later the first African American Supreme Court justice), who dismantled Jim Crow laws that denied blacks their civil rights and who won the famous 1954 case of *Brown v. Board of Education of Topeka* that toppled the prevailing "separate but equal" tradition. According to civil rights reporter and Marshall biographer Juan Williams, it was Marshall, more than anyone else, who demolished the legal foundations of segregation in America (Tucker F5). The Supreme Court, in a unanimous decision, interpreted the Fourteenth Amendment to mean that "separate is inherently unequal."

Although O'Connor had little sympathy for the civil rights movement, she disliked Southern segregationists as much as self-righteous Northern reformers. Like William Faulkner, she hated being mocked by people who did not understand the South. She felt, for instance, that Eudora Welty's anti-racist story "Where Is the Voice Coming From?" in the *New Yorker* would be misunderstood by "all the stupid Yankee liberals." She wrote a friend about her annoyance, concluding "a plague on everybody's house as far as the race business goes" (Wood 92–93). Her friends' anecdotes show that O'Connor supported black causes: She declared that she became an integrationist when she first heard a white bus driver ridicule African American passengers and order them to the back of the bus (Wood 94).

During the height of the civil rights struggle in 1963, however, O'Connor doubted that the integration battle would define a new type of literature. "The Negro will in the matter of a few years have his constitutional rights and we will all then see that the business of getting along with each other is much the same as it has always been, even though new manners are called for. The fiction writer is interested in individuals, not races; he knows that good and evil are not apportioned along racial lines . . ." (Magee 109).

Most states complied with public school integration, but the South resisted. Southern members of Congress condemned the Court's decision, and white citizens' groups rallied to continue segregation. Some Southern states permitted public funds to be used to support so-called private schools. When the court ordered the integration of the University of Alabama in 1956, whites rioted. Uncertain that the government should promote civil rights, President Eisenhower refused to endorse the Supreme Court's decision. However, in the fall of 1957 an explosive situation in Little Rock, Arkansas, forced him to act. After Governor Orval Faubus dramatically stood at the Central High School door to block the entrance of black students and riots errupted, protesting school desegregation, the President sent federal troops to quell the mob violence and to enforce the Court's order.

Civil rights in the 1950s gained momentum in other areas as well. In 1955, when the revised version of "A Good Man Is Hard to Find" was published, a black woman, Rosa Parks, inadvertently instigated the Montgomery, Alabama, bus boycott when she would not relinquish her seat to a white passenger. Parks later explained simply that she kept her seat because her feet were tired. After Dr. Martin Luther King Jr. led nearly forty thousand African Americans in their refusal to ride the buses, officials finally accepted a court order to integrate city transportation. In the following years, nonviolent sit-ins at lunch counters spread throughout the South, and people of all races battled together to overturn the long-held, conservative institutions of racial inequality.

By 1960 the stereotypes of blacks as poor, lazy, and illiterate began to fade, as shown in O'Connor's extensive correspondence with her Northern liberal friend Maryat Lee. These letters reflect O'Connor's views on race. As a writer living in New York City, but frequently visiting Milledgeville, Lee gave O'Connor a wider perspective on the issues of integration, blacks' upward mobility, and civil rights protests. She wrote the following to O'Connor in 1960:

> In the subway I sat beside three colored men, dressed in beautiful expensive and very conservative clothes—doctors or lawyers or what, and one was reading The Status Seekers. The news from down there [evidently concerning Martin Luther King and the Civil Rights Movement] is impressive. A bloodless well not so bloodless revolution is going on it would seem if anyone pays heed to the Papers. (Gordon 27)

Indeed, the civil rights movement is the topic of several letters O'Connor and Lee exchanged, and as Sarah Gordon proves, the correspondence shows the genesis of O'Connor's only story dealing directly with race, "Everything That Rises Must Converge." Although O'Connor "may not have been as enlightened about race as we would like for her to have been," Gordon asserts, "we must nonetheless acknowledge the power of her observation that a smug trust in human goodness is doomed" (35).

POPULAR CULTURE IN THE EARLY FIFTIES

Conservatism extended beyond business, social, and political issues; the literary culture was also rather conservative. For example, O'Connor's readers often failed to understand her work because of rigid stereotypes about Southerners and women writers. When novelist and critic Evelyn Waugh remarked about her stories, "If these are in fact the work of a young lady, they are indeed remarkable," he showed his astonishment that a woman wrote the collection *A Good Man Is Hard to Find* (Giroux xii). Another critic bewildered by her writing was a *Time* reviewer, who called the collection "ten witheringly sarcastic stories" by a "talented Southern lady whose work is highly unladylike." Describing O'Connor's Southern characters as "maimed souls" moving along an updated Tobacco Road, the reviewer relied on other clichés. O'Connor, wrote the critic, strips "the acres ofclay-country individuality with the merciless efficiency of a cotton-picking machine. . . . Her instruments are a brutal irony, a slam-bang humor and a style of writing as balefully direct as a death sentence." Oblivious to O'Connor's serious religious theme, the *Time* critic depicted the grandmother as a "babbling old feather-wit" then asserted that O'Connor "packs a punch" with "sheer sardonic brutality" (*Time* 114). In a society less enlightened about women's equal abilities, and more bound by rigid preconceptions of gender roles, her contemporaries often saw her use of violence and irony as decidedly "unladylike."

Afflicted with lupus, a degenerative immune system disease, O'Connor stayed home most of the time. She never held a full-time job, never married, and never had children. However, she made many trips to give lectures, and she maintained contacts through her voluminous correspondence. In 1961 she received a portable television from some nuns in gratitude for her getting their book, *A Memoir of Mary Ann,* published. In her humorous voice she wrote to a friend, "So me and ma have entered the twentieth century at last. I can now tell you all about Geritol, Pepto-Bismol, Anacin, Bufferin, any kind of soap or floor wax . . ." (Fitzgerald, *HB* 435). She enjoyed television—especially the educational channel—because the new mass medium provided her another view of world affairs as well as human idiosyncrasies.

O'Connor shrewdly observed life as portrayed by the media; in fact, she refers to popular culture in "A Good Man Is Hard to Find." June Star alludes to the popular contest show *Queen for a Day.* Patti Page's country-and-western song "The Tennessee Waltz" plays on the nickelodeon at Red Sammy's. The grandmother jokes about *Gone With the Wind,* by Atlanta writer Margaret Mitchell. And, of course, the blues song "A Good Man Is Hard to Find," made famous by Bessie Smith, supplies the story's title. These references to popular culture establish the story's realistic setting in 1950s Georgia as certainly as the mother's headkerchief and grandmother's white gloves set the tone of ladylike characterization.

THE SOUTH: A SENSE OF PLACE

O'Connor's universal themes transcend the South, but her focus is on her region. O'Connor's hometown of Milledgeville offers readers a sense of place. Capital of Georgia from 1807 to 1868, the town has an antebellum governor's mansion reminiscent of the South's glory days. The grandmother in O'Connor's story recalls these times past-scenes of beautiful plantation homes with white columns, manicured lawns, and springtime gardens full of blooming azaleas and dogwood. However, O'Connor would have warned against categorizing the South with clichés. In *Dixie Rising* (1997), Peter Applebome analyzes the effects of the South on American culture. For a definitive statement, he turns to O'Connor, whom he calls "the foremost chronicler of an archgothic South drenched in sin and redemption." Applebome quotes her essay "The Regional Writer" which declares that the South's identity is "not really connected with mocking-birds and beaten biscuits and white columns anymore than it is with hookworm and bare feet and muddy clay roads. . . . It is not made from what passes, but from those qualities that endure . . ." (25).

The Southern landscape O'Connor knew best is found at her home, Andalusia, about five miles outside Milledgeville. In the 1950s the farm had some 500 acres with cattle, horses, and peacocks. Critic Granville Hicks visited O'Connor in 1962 and described in the *Saturday Review* his being awe-struck by her many proud peacocks: "They are everywhere one looks, the cocks strutting about the yard and crying out at us from shed roofs, and periodically, for this is the right season, spreading their incredible tails" (22). O'Connor adored these peafowl: they symbolize spirituality and mystery in her story "The Displaced Person."

Southern white Christians dominate O'Connor's fictional landscape. Sometimes the writer mentions "Negroes," using the language that reflects her upbringing and her time—a time in which "Negro" was the standard term used by Northerners and Southerners alike. Yet O'Connor in her stories calls a plaster lawn jockey an "artificial nigger" and a black child, a "pickaninny." In fact, the traditions of the Old South shaped O'Connor's language so definitively that her letters to friends include certain racial epithets, words she had heard all her life. But even in the 1950s she would not have used the offensive words in her public voice. When the grandmother in the story refers to a "cute little pickaninny," O'Connor's narrative voice follows with references to the "little Negro." This genteel sensibility in her public persona is explained in her letters. She writes a friend that for a public reading of "A Good Man Is Hard to Find," she planned to delete the part "about the little nigger who doesn't have any britches on. . . . I can write with ease what I forbear to read" (Fitzgerald, *HB* 317).

To put this racial epithet in proper context, one can look at William Faulkner's "A Rose for Emily" and Mark Twain's *Adventures of Huckleberry Finn*. "Nigger" has the power to offend, but most critics see this choice of language as appropriate to characters in a particular time and place. Faulkner refers to the sense of place as the little postage stamp of native soil that gives one a sense of identity.

Similarly, O'Connor's Old South upbringing molded her way of thinking and grounded her characters in time and place. She admitted that she used only parts of her Southern community to make her points as a writer.

"You know, people say that Southern life is not the way you picture it. Well, Lord help us. Let's hope not" (Magee 70). O'Connor appreciated her Southern heritage and culture: "Southern writers are stuck with the South and it's a good thing to be stuck with" (Magee 108). Furthermore, she proudly affirmed the unique character of the South—a cultural identity she wished would not change:

> The anguish that most of us have observed for some time now has been caused not by the fact that the South is alienated from the rest of the country, but by the fact that it is not alienated enough, that every day we are getting more and more like the rest of the country, that we are being forced out, not only of our many sins, but of our few virtues. (Reed and Reed 294)

VIOLENCE IN THE SOUTH

When the battle over civil rights erupted into violence in the South, some people assumed that violence was naturally part of the Southern way of life. The South has by far the highest murder rate in the United States, according to scholars who study the region's character. Their documentation shows that the eleven states of the former Confederacy all rank in the top twenty states for homicide. In fact, the South has had the highest murder rate (almost double that of the Northeast) ever since the nineteenth century, when records of homicides by region were begun (Butterfield A8). Roger Lane's 1997 *Murder in America: A History* asserts that murders in the South often result from quarrels between acquaintances or fights between lovers or family members. This legacy of violent behavior comes in part from the Scotch-Irish immigrants who heavily populated the backcountry regions of the South. David Hackett Fisher, Brandeis University professor of history, explains that these settlers had a culture based on centuries of fighting between the kings of England and Scotland over their borderlands, as well as a tough determination to protect honor and reputation. Indeed, America has historically tolerated, even admired, the sort of aggression that leads to violence. Scholars often point to the South's poverty and weak law enforcement as other contributing factors to the region's violence (Butterfield A8).

Just as art often imitates reality, so O'Connor defends the violence in her fiction by reminding people of the murder and mayhem found in newspapers every day. Her second novel, *The Violent Bear It Away* (1960), reflects her concern with the violence as a prelude to religious experience. Although strangers commit the murders in "A Good Man Is Hard to Find," common knowledge of the high rate of Southern homicide makes believable a social outcast who would murder innocent people who happened to be in the wrong place at the wrong time.

Because Southerners suffered defeat in war, they felt stigmatized as outcasts. O'Connor believed, however, that losing the Civil War served to create the South's distinctive character. Being the nation's "Misfit," the South established a firm sense of regional unity. As heir to the Southern renaissance, O'Connor continued the literary tradition by including a strong sense of place and awareness of spirituality, albeit tainted by violence. Her letters and essays explain her particular intentions in her art. In "The Fiction Writer & His Country" O'Connor asserts that the novelist with Christian concerns may be "forced to take ever more violent means" to get the artistic vision across to an audience not believing in God (*MM* 33–34). Thus, she uses violence to illuminate the religious themes central to her fiction.

RELIGION IN THE SOUTH

In a letter dated November 6, 1955 (soon after publication of *A Good Man Is Hard to Find*), O'Connor states, "I write the way I do because and only because I am a Catholic. I feel that if I were not a Catholic, I would have no reason to write, no reason to see, no reason ever to feel horrified or even to enjoy anything" (Fitzgerald, *HB* 114).

As a devout Roman Catholic living in predominantly Protestant Georgia, O'Connor neither apologized for her religion nor felt she was a misfit. On the contrary, her religion gave purpose to her writing and expanded her creative freedom. She was born a Catholic, went to Catholic schools in her early years, and never wished to leave the Church (Fitzgerald, *HB* 114). Her fiction was a concrete expression of life's mystery, allowing her to explore the difficulty of religious belief. She shaped her fictional world according to three basic Christian theological truths: the Fall, Redemption, and Judgment. As Robert Fitzgerald asserts, her stories "became, for her, a way of testing and defining and conveying that superior knowledge that must be called religious" (May 400).

"A Good Man Is Hard to Find" focuses on The Misfit's being haunted by the choice between Jesus and the devil, belief and nonbelief. The title's allusion to the popular blues song also recalls the ultimate mystery of Christian life: that is, religious faith comes through the ultimate good man, Christ. O'Connor believed the South may not always be "Christ-centered," but it was most certainly "Christ-haunted" (Magee 12). At the heart of this story lies the search for spirituality amid disbelief. Because she thought her nonbelieving readers could not accept that vision, she uses violence to get the attention of unbelievers because, as O'Connor explains, "to the hard-of-hearing you shout, and for the almost-blind you draw large and startling figures"(*MM* 34). If the senseless deaths in "A Good Man Is Hard to Find" shock readers enough to consider life's mysteries, O'Connor would have accomplished her purpose. In fact, at a public reading of the story, she urged college students to forget the dead bodies—to go beyond the literal account of a family murdered—to understand the story as a spiritual account of "the action of grace" in the grandmother's soul (*MM* 113). While some scholars proclaimed God dead in the post-Holocaust world, O'Connor held steadfast to her faith. When an interviewer asked about her main concerns as a writer, O'Connor replied, "I will admit to certain preoccupations that I get, I suppose, because I'm a Catholic; preoccupations with belief and with death and grace and the devil . . . (Magee 103). Furthermore, she said that her fictional preoccupation with violence is often "technical" and that others could see things in her stories she could not "because if I did see I would be too frightened to write them" (Fitzgerald, *HB* 149).

This firm religious belief points to a commonly held assumption that Southerners tend to be more religious than Americans in general. According to surveys, more Southerners than non-Southerners believe in God, and people who move to the South become more religious. As one study concludes, "Something about the South as a cultural environment . . . encourages higher levels of religiosity." University of Florida religion professor Samuel S. Hill, agrees: "In the South, religion is upper case. . . . It's God, capital G, Christ, capital C, and Prayer, capital P." Also affirming this viewpoint, a Baptist minister in Raleigh, North Carolina, explains, "Generally in the South, and particularly in the African American community, there is a tenaciousness to the Word. . . . Heaven and hell are real in our tradition; creation is real in our tradition, and Satan is a spiritual force." Compared to Northerners, Southerners tend to have a greater intensity about their religious convictions, more willingly accept the Bible as a moral standard for values, and more definitely lean toward religious conservatism ("Lord, yes" A5).

As O'Connor explains in her essay "The Catholic Novelist in the Protestant South," the "vital strength" of Southern literature and the Southern identity comes from "those beliefs and qualities which she [the South] has absorbed from the Scriptures and from her own history of defeat and violation: a distrust of the abstract, a sense of human dependence on the grace of God, and a knowledge that evil is not simply a problem to be solved, but a mystery to be endured" (*MM* 209).

O'Connor's Relevance Today

These cultural traditions, along with various historical and social events, bring O'Connor's world into sharper focus as background for your reading "A Good Man Is Hard to Find." The story's truths about moral values and religious faith still resonate. Because of O'Connor's universal themes, her literary reputation has soared since her death in 1964. Film adaptations of her work, such as *The Displaced Person* (1979) and *Wise Blood* (1980), and a wealth of books and articles have enhanced her popularity with a larger audience. Despite her modest canon, O'Connor remains a major American short story writer today.

Works Consulted

Applebome, Peter. *Dixie Rising: How the South Is Shaping American Values, Politics, and Culture.* San Diego: Harcourt, 1997.

Asals, Frederick. Introduction. *"A Good Man Is Hard to Find."* Women Writers: Text and Contexts Ser. New Brunswick, NJ: Rutgers UP, 1993. 3–25.

Blum, John M., et al. *The National Experience: A History of the United States.* 6th ed. San Diego: Harcourt, 1985.

Butterfield, Fox. "South mixes honor and homicide." *State* [Columbia, SC] 26 July 1998: A8.

Fitzgerald, Robert. Introduction. *Everything That Rises Must Converge.* New York: Noonday, 1966. vii–xxxiv.

Fitzgerald, Sally. Introduction. *The Habit of Being: Letters of Flannery O'Connor.* New York: Farrar, 1979. ix–xvii. [cited as *HB*]

Giroux, Robert. Introduction. *The Complete Stories of Flannery O'Connor.* New York: Farrar, 1971. vii–xvii.

Gordon, Sarah. "Maryat and Julian and the 'not so bloodless revolution.'" *Flannery O'Connor Bulletin* 21 (1992): 25–36.

Hicks, Granville. "A Writer at Home with Her Heritage." *Saturday Review* 29 May 1965: 22–23.

Lane, Roger. *Murder in America: A History.* The History of Crime and Criminal Justice Ser. Columbus: Ohio State UP, 1997.

"Lord, yes: South's religious faith still strong, poll says." *State* [Columbia, SC] 31 July 1998: A5.

Magee, Rosemary M. *Conversations with Flannery O'Connor.* Jackson: UP of Mississippi, 1987.

May, John R. "Flannery O'Connor." *The New Consciousness, 1941–1968. Concise Dictionary of American Literary Biography.* Detroit: Gale, 1987. 399–407.

O'Connor, Flannery. "The Fiction Writer & His Country." *Mystery and Manners: Occasional Prose.* Ed. Sally and Robert Fitzgerald. New York: Farrar, 1969. 25–35. [cited as *MM*]

Reed, John Shelton, and Dale Volberg Reed. *1001 Things Everyone Should Know about the South.* New York: Doubleday, 1996.

"Such Nice People." Rev. of *A Good Man Is Hard to Find. Time* 6 June 1955: 114.

Tucker, Cynthia. "Author paints incomplete, but compelling picture of Thurgood Marshall." Rev. of *Thurgood Marshall: American Revolutionary* by Juan Williams. *State* [Columbia, SC] 1 Nov. 1998: F5.

Wood, Ralph. "Where Is the Voice Coming From? Flannery O'Connor on Race." *Flannery O'Connor Bulletin* 22 (1993–94): 90–118.

Literature

About the Author

FLANNERY O'CONNOR (1925–1964) died before the age of forty, but she left a rich legacy of thirty-one short stories, two novels, many essays and book reviews, and hundreds of letters. She had totally committed herself to her writing even before she was diagnosed with lupus, as she explains in a 1953 letter. "My father had [lupus] some twelve or fifteen years ago but at that time there was nothing for it but the undertaker; now it can be controlled with ACTH. I have enough energy to write with and as that is all I have any business doing anyhow, I can with one eye squinted take it all as a blessing. What you have to measure out, you come to observe closer or so I tell myself" (Fitzgerald, *HB* 57).

Born in Savannah, Georgia, on March 25, 1925, Mary Flannery O'Connor was the only child of Regina Cline and Edward Francis O'Connor, a real estate businessman. He died of lupus when she was fifteen. Twenty-four years later, she died of the same disease. In Milledgeville, home of her mother's family for several generations, O'Connor graduated from Peabody High School in 1942, and from Georgia State College for Women (now Georgia College & State University) in 1945. She worked on the college yearbook and newspaper staffs, and in her senior year, served as editor of the literary magazine. She earned her B.A. degree in social science in just three years under the accelerated wartime curriculum. Two years later, after winning a graduate fellowship, she earned a Master of Fine Arts degree from the Writer's Workshop at the State University of Iowa. When she published "The Geranium" (1946), she dropped her first name, Mary. In the introduction to *The Complete Stories,* O'Connor's professor Paul Engle describes meeting O'Connor for the first time when she asked to be admitted into Iowa's writing program. Engle recalls that he could not understand her Southern accent at first, "but on the page her prose was imaginative, tough, alive: just like Flannery herself" (Giroux vii).

Beginning the life of an independent writer in 1947, O'Connor won the Rinehart-Iowa Fiction Award of $750 for writing her first novel, which she worked on at Yaddo, a writers' colony in Saratoga Springs, New York. On July 4, 1948, she wrote to her newly found literary agent Elizabeth McKee, "I am glad you look kindly on handling my work" (Fitzgerald, *HB* 5). Thus began a professional relationship and personal friendship that lasted throughout the rest of O'Connor's life. In these early letters O'Connor described her early publications that resulted from revision of stories in her master's thesis, *The Geranium: A Collection of Short Stories.* "Train" appeared in the prestigious *Sewanee Review* (1948), and another well-known journal, *Partisan Review,* published "The Peeler" and "The Heart of the Park" (1949). She left Yaddo in 1949, and after a short time in New York City, she moved in with Sally and Robert Fitzgerald and their family in Ridgefield, Connecticut, and continued reworking these stories for her first novel. Sally Fitzgerald describes how O'Connor seemed to walk stiffly when boarding the train home to Milledgeville in December 1950. A few days later came the shocking diagnosis of lupus. In spite of her hospitalization for high fevers and her daily cortisone drug treatments, she continued to revise her novel *Wise Blood* (1952).

For the remaining twelve years of her life, O'Connor stayed close to home at Andalusia, on the outskirts of Milledgeville, and traveled on a very limited basis. She published "A Good Man Is Hard to Find" in 1953, and after more rewriting, it became the title story for *A Good Man Is Hard to Find* (1955), a collection of ten stories dealing with sin, death, grace, and redemption. The stories in her second collection, *Everything That Rises Must Converge* (1965), all move toward a powerful climactic moment, a "convergence." *The Complete Stories* (1971) presents all her short stories in the order of their composition, thus providing insight into how her creative talents grew from the first story ("The Geranium") to the last ("Judgement Day," a revision of "The Geranium"). Because both stories focus on people deprived of their true homes, the reader sees that from the beginning to the end of her writing career, the themes of place and resurrection are crucially important. Indeed, her resolute Catholic faith defines all of her fiction.

O'Connor's work garnered many awards and honors. She received a *Kenyon Review* Fellowship in Fiction (1953), National Institute of Arts and Letters grant (1957), O. Henry Memorial Awards first prizes in 1957, 1963, and 1965; and a Ford Foundation grant (1959). After O'Connor's death on

August 3, 1964, Sally and Robert Fitzgerald edited *Mystery and Manners: Occasional Prose* (1969), a collection of O'Connor's lectures and essays that explain her views about writing fiction and about being a Catholic writer in an age of general unbelief. Awarded the National Book Critics Circle Award, *The Habit of Being: Letters of Flannery O'Connor* (1979), edited by Sally Fitzgerald, illuminates O'Connor's life and art from 1948 until her death. By selecting *The Complete Short Stories* for the National Book Award, judges made an exception, because the award had previously gone to living writers only. Despite these awards, not everyone admires O'Connor. When interviewed in 1960 by students at the College of Saint Teresa (Winona, MN), O'Connor talked about "crank letters" from her readers: "Some old lady said that my book left a bad taste in her mouth. I wrote back to her and said, 'You weren't supposed to eat it'" (Magee 60).

To a professor of English, who had written O'Connor about the symbolism of a character's name, she replied (less than two months before her death) that she was in the hospital and "not up to literary questions. . . . As for Mrs. May, I must have named her that because I knew some English teacher would write and ask me why. I think you folks sometimes strain the soup too thin . . ." (Fitzgerald, *HB* 582). Another example of her exasperation with readers too caught up in symbolism hunting is her response to a young teacher who insisted on seeing The Misfit's black hat as symbolic of Christ. O'Connor denied that interpretation, saying that most rural Georgia men wore black hats. When that answer did not suffice, O'Connor silenced the interrogator this way: "I said it was to cover his head; and after that he left me alone. Anyway, that's what's happening to the teaching of literature" (Fitzgerald, *HB* 334).

Perhaps the best introduction to the writer's short fiction is "A Good Man Is Hard to Find," her most popular story and one of the most misunderstood. In fact, every time a story of hers appeared in a freshman English anthology, O'Connor said, she feared it would be dissected like a laboratory frog with "its little organs laid open." She advised readers not to overanalyze her stories but "to forget about the enlightenment and just try to enjoy them" (*MM* 107).

A Good Man Is Hard to Find
(1955)

The grandmother didn't want to go to Florida. She wanted to visit some of her connections in east Tennessee and she was seizing at every chance to change Bailey's mind. Bailey was the son she lived with, her only boy. He was sitting on the edge of his chair at the table, bent over the orange sports section of the *Journal.* "Now look here, Bailey," she said, "see here, read this," and she stood with one hand on her thin hip and the other rattling the newspaper at his bald head. "Here this fellow that calls himself The Misfit is aloose from the Federal Pen and headed toward Florida and you read here what it says he did to these people. Just you read it. I wouldn't take my children in any direction with a criminal like that aloose in it. I couldn't answer to my conscience if I did."

Bailey didn't look up from his reading so she wheeled around then and faced the children's mother, a young woman in slacks, whose face was as broad and innocent as a cabbage and was tied around with a green headkerchief that had two points on the top like a rabbit's ears. She was sitting on the sofa, feeding the baby his apricots out of a jar. "The children have been to Florida before," the old lady said. "You all ought to take them somewhere else for a change so they would see different parts of the world and be broad. They never have been to east Tennessee."

The children's mother didn't seem to hear her but the eight-year-old boy, John Wesley, a stocky child with glasses, said, "If you don't want to go to Florida, why dontcha stay at home?" He and the little girl, June Star, were reading the funny papers on the floor.

"She wouldn't stay at home to be queen for a day," June Star said without raising her yellow head.

"Yes and what would you do if this fellow, The Misfit, caught you?" the grandmother asked.

"I'd smack his face," John Wesley said.

"She wouldn't stay at home for a million bucks," June Star said. "Afraid she'd miss something. She has to go everywhere we go."

"All right, Miss," the grandmother said. "Just remember that the next time you want me to curl your hair."

June Star said her hair was naturally curly.

The next morning the grandmother was the first one in the car, ready to go. She had her big black valise that looked like the head of a hippopotamus in one corner, and underneath it she was hiding a basket with Pitty Sing, the cat, in it. She didn't intend for the cat to be left alone in the house for three days because he would miss her too much and she was afraid he might brush against one of the gas burners and accidentally asphyxiate himself. Her son, Bailey, didn't like to arrive at a motel with a cat.

She sat in the middle of the back seat with John Wesley and June Star on either side of her. Bailey and the children's mother and the baby sat in front and they left Atlanta at eight forty-five with the mileage on the car at 55890. The grandmother wrote this down because she thought it would be interesting to say how many miles they had been when they got back. It took them twenty minutes to reach the outskirts of the city.

The old lady settled herself comfortably, removing her white cotton gloves and putting them up with her purse on the shelf in front of the back window. The children's mother still had on slacks and still had her head tied up in a green kerchief, but the grandmother had on a navy blue straw sailor hat with a bunch of white violets on the brim and a navy blue dress with a small white dot in the print. Her collars and cuffs were white organdy trimmed with lace and at her neckline she had pinned a purple spray of cloth violets containing a sachet. In case of an accident, anyone seeing her dead on the highway would know at once that she was a lady.

She said she thought it was going to be a good day for driving, neither too hot nor too cold, and she cautioned Bailey that the speed limit was fifty-five miles an hour and that the patrolmen hid themselves behind billboards and small clumps of trees and sped out after you before you had a chance to slow down. She pointed out interesting details of the scenery: Stone Mountain; the blue granite that in some places came up to both sides of the highway; the brilliant red clay banks slightly streaked with purple; and the various crops that made rows of green lace-work on the ground. The trees were full of silver-white sunlight and the meanest of them sparkled. The children were reading comic magazines and their mother had gone back to sleep.

"Let's go through Georgia fast so we won't have to look at it much," John Wesley said.

"If I were a little boy," said the grandmother, "I wouldn't talk about my native state that way. Tennessee has the mountains and Georgia has the hills."

"Tennessee is just a hillbilly dumping ground," John Wesley said, "and Georgia is a lousy state too."

"You said it," June Star said.

"In my time," said the grandmother, folding her thin veined fingers, "children were more respectful of their native states and their parents and everything else. People did right then. Oh look at the cute little pickaninny!" she said and pointed to a Negro child standing in the door of a shack. "Wouldn't that make a picture, now?" she asked and they all turned and looked at the little Negro out of the back window. He waved.

"He didn't have any britches on," June Star said.

"He probably didn't have any," the grandmother explained. "Little niggers in the country don't have things like we do. If I could paint, I'd paint that picture," she said.

The children exchanged comic books.

The grandmother offered to hold the baby and the children's mother passed him over the front seat to her. She set him on her knee and bounced him and told him about the things they were passing. She rolled her eyes and screwed up her mouth and stuck her leathery thin face into his smooth bland one. Occasionally he gave her a faraway smile. They passed a large cotton field with five or six graves fenced in the middle of it, like a small island. "Look at the graveyard!" the grandmother said, pointing it out. "That was the old family burying ground. That belonged to the plantation."

"Where's the plantation?" John Wesley asked.

"Gone With the Wind," said the grandmother. "Ha. Ha."

When the children finished all the comic books they had brought, they opened the lunch and ate it. The grandmother ate a peanut butter sandwich and an olive and would not let the children throw the box and the paper napkins out the window. When there was nothing else to do they played a game by choosing a cloud and making the other two guess what shape it suggested. John Wesley took one the shape of a cow and June Star guessed a cow and John Wesley said, no, an automobile, and June Star said he didn't play fair, and they began to slap each other over the grandmother.

The grandmother said she would tell them a story if they would keep quiet. When she told a story, she rolled her eyes and waved her head and was very dramatic. She said once when she was a maiden lady she had been courted by a Mr. Edgar Atkins Teagarden from Jasper, Georgia. She said he was a very good-looking man and a gentleman and that he brought her a watermelon every Saturday afternoon with his initials cut in it, E. A. T. Well, one Saturday, she said, Mr. Teagarden brought the watermelon and there was nobody at home and he left it on the front porch and returned in his buggy to Jasper, but she never got the watermelon, she said, because a nigger boy ate it when he saw the initials, E. A. T.! This story tickled John Wesley's funny bone and he giggled and giggled but June Star didn't think it was any good. She said she wouldn't marry a man that just brought her a watermelon on Saturday. The grandmother said she would have done well to marry Mr. Teagarden because he was a gentleman and had bought Coca-Cola stock when it first came out and that he died only a few years ago, a very wealthy man.

They stopped at The Tower for barbecued sandwiches. The Tower was a part stucco and part wood filling station and dance hall set in a clearing outside of Timothy. A fat man named Red Sammy Butts ran it and there were signs stuck here and there on the building and for miles up and down the highway saying, TRY RED SAMMY'S FAMOUS BARBECUE. NONE LIKE FAMOUS RED SAMMY'S! RED SAM! THE FAT BOY WITH THE HAPPY LAUGH. A VETERAN! RED SAMMY'S YOUR MAN!

Red Sammy was lying on the bare ground outside The Tower with his head under a truck while a gray monkey about a foot high, chained to a small chinaberry tree, chattered nearby. The monkey sprang back into the tree and got on the highest limb as soon as he saw the children jump out of the car and run toward him.

Inside, The Tower was a long dark room with a counter at one end and tables at the other and dancing space in the middle. They all sat down at a board table next to the nickelodeon and Red Sam's wife, a tall burnt-brown woman with hair and eyes lighter than her skin, came and took their order. The children's mother put a dime in the machine and played "The Tennessee Waltz," and the grandmother said that tune always made her want to dance. She asked Bailey if he would like to dance but he only glared at her. He didn't have a naturally sweet disposition like she did and trips made him nervous. The grandmother's brown eyes were very bright. She swayed her head from side to side and pretended she was dancing in her chair. June Star said play something she could tap to so the children's mother put in another dime and played a fast number and June Star stepped out onto the dance floor and did her tap routine.

"Ain't she cute?" Red Sam's wife said, leaning over the counter. "Would you like to come be my little girl?"

"No I certainly wouldn't," June Star said. "I wouldn't live in a broken-down place like this for a million bucks!" and she ran back to the table.

"Ain't she cute?" the woman repeated, stretching her mouth politely.

"Aren't you ashamed?" hissed the grandmother.

Red Sam came in and told his wife to quit lounging on the counter and hurry up with these people's order. His khaki trousers reached just to his hip bones and his stomach hung over them like a sack of meal swaying under his shirt. He came over and sat down at a table nearby and let out a combination sigh and yodel. "You can't win," he said. "You can't win," and he wiped his sweating red face off with a gray handkerchief. "These days you don't know who to trust," he said. "Ain't that the truth?"

"People are certainly not nice like they used to be," said the grandmother.

"Two fellers come in here last week," Red Sammy said, "driving a Chrysler. It was a old beat-up car but it was a good one and these boys looked all right to me. Said they worked at the mill and you know I let them fellers charge the gas they bought? Now why did I do that?"

"Because you're a good man!" the grandmother said at once.

"Yes'm, I suppose so," Red Sam said as if he were struck with this answer.

His wife brought the orders, carrying the five plates all at once without a tray, two in each hand and one balanced on her arm. "It isn't a soul in this green world of God's that you can trust," she said. "And I don't count nobody out of that, not nobody," she repeated, looking at Red Sammy.

"Did you read about that criminal, The Misfit, that's escaped?" asked the grandmother.

"I wouldn't be a bit surprised if he didn't attact this place right here," said the woman. "If he hears about it being here, I wouldn't be none surprised to see him. If he hears it's two cent in the cash register, I wouldn't be at all surprised if he . . . ."

"That'll do," Red Sam said. "Go bring these people their Co'-Colas," and the woman went off to get the rest of the order.

"A good man is hard to find," Red Sammy said. "Everything is getting terrible. I remember the day you could go off and leave your screen door unlatched. Not no more."

He and the grandmother discussed better times. The old lady said that in her opinion Europe was entirely to blame for the way things were now. She said the way Europe acted you would think we were made of money and Red Sam said it was no use talking about it, she was exactly right. The children ran outside into the white sunlight and looked at the monkey in the lacy chinaberry tree. He was busy catching fleas on himself and biting each one carefully between his teeth as if it were a delicacy.

They drove off again into the hot afternoon. The grandmother took cat naps and woke up every few minutes with her own snoring. Outside of Toombsboro she woke up and recalled an old plantation that she had visited in this neighborhood once when she was a young lady. She said the house had six white columns across the front and that there was an avenue of oaks leading up to it and two little wooden trellis arbors on either side in front where you sat down with your suitor after a stroll in the garden. She recalled exactly which road to turn off to get to it. She knew that Bailey would not be willing to lose any time looking at an old house, but the more she talked about it, the more she wanted to see it once again and find out if the little twin arbors were still standing. "There was a secret panel in this house," she said craftily, not telling the truth but wishing that she were, "and the story went that all the family silver was hidden in it when Sherman came through. but it was never found . . . ."

"Hey!" John Wesley said. "Let's go see it! We'll find it! We'll poke all the woodwork and find it! Who lives there? Where do you turn off at? Hey Pop, can't we turn off there?"

"We never have seen a house with a secret panel!" June Star shrieked. "Let's go to the house with the secret panel! Hey Pop, can't we go see the house with the secret panel!"

"It's not far from here, I know," the grandmother said. "It wouldn't take over twenty minutes."

Bailey was looking straight ahead. His jaw was as rigid as a horseshoe. "No," he said.

The children began to yell and scream that they wanted to see the house with the secret panel. John Wesley kicked the back of the front seat and June Star hung over her mother's shoulder and whined desperately into her ear that they never had any fun even on their vacation, that they could never do what THEY wanted to do. The baby began to scream and John Wesley kicked the back of the seat so hard that his father could feel the blows in his kidney.

"All right!" he shouted and drew the car to a stop at the side of the road. "Will you all shut up? Will you all just shut up for one second? If you don't shut up, we won't go anywhere."

"It would be very educational for them," the grandmother murmured.

"All right," Bailey said, "but get this: this is the only time we're going to stop for anything like this. This is the one and only time."

"The dirt road that you have to turn down is about a mile back," the grandmother directed. "I marked it when we passed."

"A dirt road," Bailey groaned.

After they had turned around and were headed toward the dirt road, the grandmother recalled other points about the house, the beautiful glass over the front doorway and the candle-lamp in the hall. John Wesley said that the secret panel was probably in the fireplace.

"You can't go inside this house," Bailey said. "You don't know who lives there."

"While you all talk to the people in front, I'll run around behind and get in a window," John Wesley suggested.

"We'll all stay in the car," his mother said.

They turned onto the dirt road and the car raced roughly along in a swirl of pink dust. The grandmother recalled the times when there were no paved roads and thirty miles was a day's journey. The dirt road was hilly and there were sudden washes in it and sharp curves on dangerous embankments. All at once they would be on a hill, looking down over the blue tops of trees for miles around, then the next minute, they would be in a red depression with the dust-coated trees looking down on them.

"This place had better turn up in a minute," Bailey said, "or I'm going to turn around."

The road looked as if no one had traveled on it in months.

"It's not much farther," the grandmother said and just as she said it, a horrible thought came to her. The thought was so embarrassing that she turned red in the face and her eyes dilated and her feet jumped up, upsetting her valise in the corner. The instant the valise moved, the newspaper top she had over the basket under it rose with a snarl and Pitty Sing, the cat, sprang onto Bailey's shoulder.

The children were thrown to the floor and their mother, clutching the baby, was thrown out the door onto the ground; the old lady was thrown into the front seat. The car turned over once and landed right-side-up in a gulch off the side of the road. Bailey remained in the driver's seat with the cat—gray-striped with a broad white face and an orange nose—clinging to his neck like a caterpillar.

As soon as the children saw they could move their arms and legs, they scrambled out of the car, shouting, "We've had an ACCIDENT!" The grandmother was curled up under the dashboard, hoping she was injured so that Bailey's wrath would not come down on her all at once. The horrible thought she had had before the accident was that the house she had remembered so vividly was not in Georgia but in Tennessee.

Bailey removed the cat from his neck with both hands and flung it out the window against the side of a pine tree. Then he got out of the car and started looking for the children's mother. She was sitting against the side of the red gutted ditch, holding the screaming baby, but she only had a cut down her face and a broken shoulder. "We've had an ACCIDENT!" the children screamed in a frenzy of delight.

"But nobody's killed," June Star said with disappointment as the grandmother limped out of the car, her hat still pinned to her head but the broken front brim standing up at a jaunty angle and the violet spray hanging off the side. They all sat down in the ditch, except the children, to recover from the shock. They were all shaking.

"Maybe a car will come along," said the children's mother hoarsely.

"I believe I have injured an organ," said the grandmother, pressing her side, but no one answered her. Bailey's teeth were clattering. He had on a yellow sport shirt with bright blue parrots designed in it and his face was as yellow as the shirt. The grandmother decided that she would not mention that the house was in Tennessee.

The road was about ten feet above and they could see only the tops of the trees on the other side of it. Behind the ditch they were sitting in there were more woods, tall and dark and deep. In a few minutes they saw a car some distance away on top of a hill, coming slowly as if the occupants were watching them. The grandmother stood up and waved both arms dramatically to attract their attention. The car continued to come on slowly, disappeared around a bend and appeared again, moving even slower, on top of the hill they had gone over. It was a big black battered hearse-like automobile. There were three men in it.

It came to a stop just over them and for some minutes, the driver looked down with a steady expressionless gaze to where they were sitting, and didn't speak. Then he turned his head and muttered something to the other two and they got out. One was a fat boy in black trousers and a red sweat shirt with a silver stallion embossed on the front of it. He moved around on the right side of them and stood staring, his mouth partly open in a kind of loose grin. The other had on khaki pants and a blue striped coat and a gray hat pulled down very low, hiding most of his face. He came around slowly on the left side. Neither spoke.

The driver got out of the car and stood by the side of it, looking down at them. He was an older man than the other two. His hair was just beginning to gray and he wore silver-rimmed spectacles that gave him a scholarly look. He had a long creased face and didn't have on any shirt or undershirt. He had on blue jeans that were too tight for him and was holding a black hat and a gun. The two boys also had guns.

"We've had an ACCIDENT!" the children screamed.

The grandmother had the peculiar feeling that the bespectacled man was someone she knew. His face was as familiar to her as if she had known him all her life but she could not recall who he was. He moved away from the car and began to come down the embankment, placing his feet carefully so that he wouldn't slip. He had on tan and white shoes and no socks, and his ankles were red and thin. "Good afternoon," he said. "I see you all had you a little spill."

"We turned over twice!" said the grandmother.

"Oncet," he corrected. "We seen it happen. Try their car and see will it run, Hiram," he said quietly to the boy with the gray hat.

"What you got that gun for?" John Wesley asked. "Watcha gonna do with that gun?"

"Lady," the man said to the children's mother, "would you mind calling them children to sit down by you? Children make me nervous. I want all you all to sit down right together there where you're at."

"What are you telling US what to do for?" June Star asked.

Behind them the line of woods gaped like a dark open mouth. "Come here," said their mother.

"Look here now," Bailey began suddenly, "we're in a predicament! We're in . . . ."

The grandmother shrieked. She scrambled to her feet and stood staring. "You're The Misfit!" she said. "I recognized you at once!"

"Yes'm," the man said, smiling slightly as if he were pleased in spite of himself to be known, "but it would have been better for all of you, lady, if you hadn't of reckernized me."

Bailey turned his head sharply and said something to his mother that shocked even the children. The old lady began to cry and The Misfit reddened.

"Lady," he said, "don't you get upset. Sometimes a man says things he don't mean. I don't reckon he meant to talk to you thataway."

"You wouldn't shoot a lady, would you?" the grandmother said and removed a clean handkerchief from her cuff and began to slap at her eyes with it.

The Misfit pointed the toe of his shoe into the ground and made a little hole and then covered it up again. "I would hate to have to," he said.

"Listen," the grandmother almost screamed, "I know you're a good man. You don't look a bit like you have common blood. I know you must come from nice people!"

"Yes mam," he said, "finest people in the world." When he smiled he showed a row of strong white teeth. "God never made a finer woman than my mother and my daddy's heart was pure gold," he said. The boy with the red sweat shirt had come around behind them and was standing with his gun at his hip. The Misfit squatted down on the ground. "Watch them children, Bobby Lee," he said. "You know they make me nervous." He looked at the six of them huddled together in front of him and he seemed to be embarrassed as if he couldn't think of anything to say. "Ain't a cloud in the sky," he remarked, looking up at it. "Don't see no sun but don't see no cloud neither."

"Yes, it's a beautiful day," said the grandmother. "Listen," she said, "you shouldn't call yourself The Misfit because I know you're a good man at heart. I can just look at you and tell."

"Hush!" Bailey yelled. "Hush! Everybody shut up and let me handle this!" He was squatting in the position of a runner about to sprint forward but he didn't move.

"I pre-chate that, lady," The Misfit said and drew a little circle in the ground with the butt of his gun.

"It'll take a half a hour to fix this here car," Hiram called, looking over the raised hood of it.

"Well, first you and Bobby Lee get him and that little boy to step over yonder with you," The Misfit said, pointing to Bailey and John Wesley. "The boys want to ast you something," he said to Bailey. "Would you mind stepping back in them woods there with them?"

"Listen," Bailey began, "we're in a terrible predicament! Nobody realizes what this is," and his voice cracked. His eyes were as blue and intense as the parrots in his shirt and he remained perfectly still.

The grandmother reached up to adjust her hat brim as if she were going to the woods with him but it came off in her hand. She stood staring at it and after a second she let it fall on the ground. Hiram pulled Bailey up by the arm as if he were assisting an old man. John Wesley caught hold of his father's hand and Bobby Lee followed. They went off toward the woods and just as they reached the dark edge, Bailey turned and supporting himself against a gray naked pine truck, he shouted, "I'll be back in a minute, Mamma, wait on me!"

"Come back this instant!" his mother shrilled but they all disappeared into the woods.

"Bailey Boy!" the grandmother called in a tragic voice but she found she was looking at The Misfit squatting on the ground in front of her. "I just know you're a good man," she said desperately. "You're not a bit common!"

"Nome, I ain't a good man," The Misfit said after a second as if he had considered her statement carefully, "but I ain't the worst in the world neither. My daddy said I was a different breed of dog from my brothers and sisters. 'You know,' Daddy said, 'it's some that can live their whole life out without asking about it and it's others has to know why it is, and this boy is one of the latters. He's going to be into everything!'" He put on his black hat and looked up suddenly and then away deep into the woods as if he were embarrassed again. "I'm sorry I don't have on a shirt before you ladies," he said, hunching his shoulders slightly. "We buried our clothes that we had on when we escaped and we're just making do until we can get better. We borrowed these from some folks we met," he explained.

"That's perfectly all right," the grandmother said. "Maybe Bailey has an extra shirt in his suitcase."

"I'll look and see terrectly," the Misfit said.

"Where are they taking him?" the children's mother screamed.

"Daddy was a card himself," The Misfit said. "You couldn't put anything over on him. He never got in trouble with the Authorities though. Just had the knack of handling them."

"You could be honest too if you'd only try," said the grandmother. "Think how wonderful it would be to settle down and live a comfortable life and not have to think about somebody chasing you all the time."

The Misfit kept scratching in the ground with the butt of his gun as if he were thinking about it. "Yes'm, somebody is always after you," he murmured.

The grandmother noticed how thin his shoulder blades were just behind his hat because she was standing up looking down on him. "Do you ever pray?" she asked.

He shook his head. All she saw was the black hat wiggle between his shoulder blades. "Nome," he said.

There was a pistol shot from the woods, followed closely by another. Then silence. The old lady's head jerked around. She could hear the wind move through the tree tops like a long satisfied insuck of breath. "Bailey Boy!" she called.

"I was a gospel singer for a while," The Misfit said. "I been most everything. Been in the arm service, both land and sea, at home and abroad, been twict married, been an undertaker, been with the railroads, plowed Mother Earth, been in a tornado, seen a man burnt alive oncet," and he looked up at the children's mother and the little girl who were sitting close together, their faces white and their eyes glassy; "I even seen a woman flogged," he said.

"Pray, pray," the grandmother began, "pray, pray . . ."

"I never was a bad boy that I remember of," The Misfit said in an almost dreamy voice, "but somewheres along the line I done something wrong and got sent to the penitentiary. I was buried alive," and he looked up and held her attention to him by a steady stare.

"That's when you should have started to pray," she said. "What did you do to get sent to the penitentiary that first time?"

"Turn to the right, it was a wall," The Misfit said, looking up again at the cloudless sky. "Turn to the left, it was a wall. Look up it was a ceiling, look down it was a floor. I forget what I done, lady. I set there and set there, trying to remember what it was I done and I ain't recalled it to this day. Oncet in a while, I would think it was coming to me, but it never come."

"Maybe they put you in by mistake," the old lady said vaguely.

"Nome," he said. "It wasn't no mistake. They had the papers on me."

"You must have stolen something," she said.

The Misfit sneered slightly. "Nobody had nothing I wanted," he said. "It was a head-doctor at the penitentiary said what I had done was kill my daddy but I known that for a lie. My daddy died in nineteen ought nineteen of the epidemic flu and I never had a thing to do with it. He was buried in the Mount Hopewell Baptist churchyard and you can go there and see for yourself."

"If you would pray," the old lady said, "Jesus would help you."

"That's right," The Misfit said.

"Well then, why don't you pray?" she asked trembling with delight suddenly.

"I don't want no hep," he said. "I'm doing all right by myself."

Bobby Lee and Hiram came ambling back from the woods. Bobby Lee was dragging a yellow shirt with bright blue parrots in it.

"Thow me that shirt, Bobby Lee," The Misfit said. The shirt came flying at him and landed on his shoulder and he put it on. The grandmother couldn't name what the shirt reminded her of. "No, lady," The Misfit said while he was buttoning it up, "I found out the crime don't matter. You can do one thing or you can do another, kill a man or take a tire off his car, because sooner or later you're going to forget what it was you done and just be punished for it."

The children's mother had begun to make heaving noises as if she couldn't get her breath. "Lady," he asked, "would you and that little girl like to step off yonder with Bobby Lee and Hiram and join your husband?"

"Yes, thank you," the mother said faintly. Her left arm dangled helplessly and she was holding the baby, who had gone to sleep, in the other. "Hep that lady up, Hiram," The Misfit said as she struggled to climb out of the ditch, "and Bobby Lee, you hold onto that little girl's hand."

"I don't want to hold hands with him," June Star said. "He reminds me of a pig."

The fat boy blushed and laughed and caught her by the arm and pulled her off into the woods after Hiram and her mother.

Alone with The Misfit, the grandmother found that she had lost her voice. There was not a cloud in the sky nor any sun. There was nothing around her but woods. She wanted to tell him that he must pray. She opened and closed her mouth several times before anything came out. Finally she found herself saying, "Jesus, Jesus," meaning, Jesus will help you, but the way she was saying it, it sounded as if she might be cursing.

"Yes'm," The Misfit said as if he agreed. "Jesus thown everything off balance. It was the same case with Him as with me except He hadn't committed any crime and they could prove I had committed one because they had the papers on me. Of course," he said, "they never shown me my papers. That's why I sign myself now. I said long ago, you get a signature and sign everything you do and keep a copy of it. Then you'll know what you done and you can hold up the crime to the punishment and see do they match and in the end you'll have something to prove you ain't been treated right. I call myself The Misfit," he said, "because I can't make what all I done wrong fit what all I gone through in punishment."

There was a piercing scream from the woods, followed closely by a pistol report. "Does it seem right to you, lady, that one is punished a heap and another ain't punished at all?"

"Jesus!" the old lady cried. "You've got good blood! I know you wouldn't shoot a lady! I know you come from nice people! Pray! Jesus, you ought not to shoot a lady! I'll give you all the money I've got!"

"Lady," The Misfit said, looking beyond her far into the woods, "there never was a body that give the undertaker a tip."

There were two more pistol reports and the grandmother raised her head like a parched old turkey hen crying for water and called, "Bailey Boy, Bailey Boy!" as if her heart would break.

"Jesus was the only One that ever raised the dead," The Misfit continued, "and He shouldn't have done it. He thown everything off balance. If He did what He said, then it's nothing for you to do but thow away everything and follow Him, and if He didn't, then it's nothing for you to do but enjoy the few minutes you got left the best way you can—by killing somebody or burning down his house or doing some other meanness to him. No pleasure but meanness," he said and his voice became almost a snarl.

"Maybe He didn't raise the dead," the old lady mumbled, not knowing what she was saying and feeling so dizzy that she sank down in the ditch with her legs twisted under her.

"I wasn't there so I can't say He didn't," The Misfit said. "I wisht I had of been there," he said, hitting the ground with his fist. "It ain't right

I wasn't there because if I had of been there I would of known. Listen, lady," he said in a high voice, "if I had of been there I would of known and I wouldn't be like I am now." His voice seemed about to crack and the grandmother's head cleared for an instant. She saw the man's face twisted close to her own as if he were going to cry and she murmured, "Why you're one of my babies. You're one of my own children!" She reached out and touched him on the shoulder. The Misfit sprang back as if a snake had bitten him and shot her three times through the chest. Then he put his gun down on the ground and took off his glasses and began to clean them.

Hiram and Bobby Lee returned from the woods and stood over the ditch, looking down at the grandmother who half sat and half lay in a puddle of blood with her legs crossed under her like a child's and her face smiling up at the cloudless sky.

Without his glasses, The Misfit's eyes were red-rimmed and pale and defenseless-looking. "Take her off and thow her where you thown the others," he said, picking up the cat that was rubbing itself against his leg.

"She was a talker, wasn't she?" Bobby Lee said, sliding down the ditch with a yodel.

"She would of been a good woman," The Misfit said, "if it had been somebody there to shoot her every minute of her life."

"Some fun!" Bobby Lee said.

"Shut up, Bobby Lee," The Misfit said. "It's no real pleasure in life."

Discussion Questions

1. What interpretations of the title "A Good Man Is Hard to Find" can you suggest? Consider different meanings, starting from specific references in the story and moving from allusions to the blues song and the popular use of clichés to the more abstract possibilities that reinforce O'Connor's religious vision.

2. How does O'Connor foreshadow the death of the family?

3. What names, locations, and objects suggest greater significance than their literal meanings? Explain how these names of people, places, and things relate to the overall theme of the story.

4. What significance do you attribute to the names of the minor characters even the cat? Why are the grandmother and The Misfit unnamed?

5. Who is the story's protagonist? antagonist? Explain.

6. Who is ultimately to blame for the murders? Explain.

7. Do you think people today are more religious or less religious than people in the 1950s? O'Connor stated that she wrote for an audience that did not share her strong religious beliefs. Why does a writer use violence? Explain various possibilities, and cite specific authors and works as examples.

8. How realistic is this story of escaped criminals who wantonly murder an innocent family who just happen to be in the wrong place at the wrong time? Are the characters realistic? Are the family members to be pitied? Are some of them less worthy of sympathy than others? Explain, using specific examples of dialogue and actions.

9. Explain what The Misfit means when he says, "She would of been a good woman . . . if it had been somebody there to shoot her every minute of her life" and "It's no real pleasure in life."

10. What does this story imply about family and social values? Beyond the cliché "A good man is hard to find," what other sayings come to mind?

11. What will happen to The Misfit? Create a short narrative about his fate. For instance, he becomes a good man after all, since he had once been a gospel singer and is now haunted by and obsessed with Christ. Or, he will be captured and executed as a serial killer.

12. Alice Walker notes that some students resist reading O'Connor because she is "too difficult" or because they do not share her religious "persuasion." Explain how you personally respond to your reading of "A Good Man Is Hard to Find."

Research Topics

1. O'Connor has stated that her stories deal with conversion, changes in a character, and, more specifically, the action of grace on a character. Compare "A Good Man Is Hard to Find" with other O'Connor stories, such as "The River" and "Greenleaf," that deal with sin, grace, and redemption, as you analyze these stories' themes, settings, styles, and characterization.

2. Analyze the use of place names in "A Good Man Is Hard to Find." Find each place on a map of Georgia. The one place you will not find is Timothy. Read the pastoral letter found in I Timothy (New Testament) and suggest how this Biblical source enhances your understanding of the story.

3. When asked how it felt to be writing in the South in the shadow of the famous William Faulkner, O'Connor modestly shunned the comparison, commenting that nobody "wants his mule and wagon stalled on the same track the *Dixie Limited* is roaring down" (Reed and Reed 143). Compare "A Good Man Is Hard to Find" with one of Faulkner's stories, such as "A Rose for Emily" or "Barn Burning." Analyze the ways both writers depict their Southern characters.

4. Read various views on the characteristics that define the Southern literary tradition. Critics have compared O'Connor with many other Southerners (besides Faulkner), such as Eudora Welty and Walker Percy. Choose a well-known Southern story to compare to "A Good Man Is Hard to Find." Argue a case for your deciding which one more closely fits the "Southern tradition," based on scholars' definitions of that tradition. One accessible and entertaining source is *1001 Things Everyone Should Know about the South* (Reed and Reed, "Characteristics of Southern Literature," 140–143).

5. Analyze various Southern stereotypes in this story: the language, the characters, perhaps even the violence. Does O'Connor present a realistic portrait of a certain element of the South in the 1950s?

6. Read Ralph C. Wood's "Where Is the Voice Coming From? Flannery O'Connor on Race" (Flannery O'Connor Bulletin) and Alice Walker's essay "Beyond the Peacock" (95–108) Then analyze the racial stereotypes in "A Good Man Is Hard to Find" and perhaps in O'Connor's "The Artificial Nigger" and "Everything That Rises Must Converge." Explain exactly how O'Connor's fiction reflects attitudes about race. Argue whether or not you consider O'Connor the writer (as seen in her stories)

to be racist. What about O'Connor the individual, as seen in her letters to friends in *The Habit of Being*?

7. Examine the role of The Misfit as an outcast and compare him to other "misfit" or antisocial characters in literature. For instance, The Misfit says, "I can't make what all I done wrong fit what all I gone through in punishment." Similarly, Oedipus (in Sophocles's *Oedipus the King*) states, "I / Suffered those deeds more than I acted them, [and] My punishment [was] too great for what I had done." O'Connor lived with the Fitzgeralds before she wrote "A Good Man Is Hard to Find" and knew Robert Fitzgerald's 1941 translation of *Oedipus at Colonus*, the source for this quotation.

Secondary Sources

FREDERICK ASALS

Flannery O'Connor:
The Imagination of Extremity
(1982)

"A Good Man Is Hard to Find" continues to be O'Connor's best-known work, the story most often chosen to represent her in anthologies now as during her lifetime. Yet, fine as it is, it is not self-evidently her best story: something more than quality must account for its repeated selection by textbook editors. One reason for its popularity may well be precisely that "A Good Man Is Hard to Find" writes large the representative O'Connor themes and methods—comedy, violence, theological concern—and thus makes them quickly and unmistakably available. But another, surely, is the primordial appeal of the story, for "A Good Man Is Hard to Find" captures a very old truth, that in the midst of life we are in death, in its most compelling modern form. The characteristic contemporary nightmare of the sudden onslaught of violent death, a death that chooses its victims without warning, impersonally, apparently at random, without either motivation or remorse, the victims helpless either to escape or to defend themselves—this scenario for some of our deepest, most instinctual fears is the very basis of the story and the source of its immediate hold on our imaginations.

Interestingly enough, O'Connor's own public remarks on the story dismiss this level almost entirely. Stressing its spiritual implications, she emphasizes the grandmother's final action while brushing aside everything that leads up to it, saying, "If I took out this gesture and what she says with it, I would have no story. What was left would not be worth your attention." Her advice to readers of "A Good Man Is Hard to Find" is, "You should be on the lookout for such things as the action of grace in the Grandmother's soul, and not for the dead bodies" (*Mystery and Manners* 112–13).

This is all very high-minded, but it would seem a little difficult for the unprejudiced reader of "A Good Man Is Hard to Find" to ignore the dead bodies, and while one may agree with O'Connor that the story is "something more than an account of a family murdered on the way to Florida" (*Mystery and Manners,* 114), it surely is, most immediately, just that "account." Any full discussion of the story must deal with both the grandmother's soul and the dead bodies, and indeed with the tension between the two levels implied here, for that tension is at the very heart of the story.

It is The Misfit who, in stating his own dilemma, articulates the story's central metaphor in the most frequently quoted passage from O'Connor's fiction:

> "Jesus was the only One ever raised the dead," The Misfit continued, "and He shouldn't have done it. He thown everything off balance. If He did what He said, then it's nothing for you to do but thow away everything and follow Him, and if he didn't, then it's nothing for you to do but enjoy the few minutes you got left the best way you can—by killing somebody or burning down his house or doing some other meanness to him. No pleasure but meanness," he said and his voice had become almost a snarl.

In every sense, "A Good Man Is Hard to Find" dramatizes a world radically off balance. Precisely at the center of the story a pleasure trip to Florida suddenly becomes an extended encounter with death when the family's car flips over, thereby slicing the action of the story neatly in half. O'Connor makes no attempt to mask the melodrama of this turning point; indeed, she insists on it by having the children shriek not once but three times ("in a frenzy of delight"), "We've had an ACCIDENT!". It is left to the reader to try to reconcile the two halves of the story, to make them balance around this pivotal act.

And on the most obvious level, that of action, the two sections remain resolutely off balance. The first half of "A Good Man Is Hard to Find" is apparently as random and purposeless as the lives of the family it focuses on: they are headed for Florida, but, as episode succeeds episode, it is far less clear where the story is headed. The characters talk on diverse topics, quibble, make observations on the scenery, the children play a game, the grandmother tells a story, they stop for lunch, June Star tap dances, and so on. As a mimetic technique, the impression of fragmentation in the opening half of the story is O'Connor's way of establishing the discordance and emptiness of their superficial lives. Beneath the surface, however, this section has a greater coherence than first appears. The silent juxtaposition of apparently unrelated episodes both further reveals their, and especially the grandmother's, values and binds this part of the story more firmly together on a level beyond action. Consider the following examples of one episode giving way to another so that the second forms an ironic comment on the first:

> "In my time," said the grandmother, folding her thin veined fingers, "children were more respectful of their native states and their parents and everything else. People did right then. *Oh look at the cute little pickaninny!" she said and pointed to a Negro child standing in the door of a shack.*

> He [Red Sammy] and the grandmother discussed better times. The old lady said that in her opinion Europe was entirely to blame for the way things were now. She said the way Europe acted you would think we were made of money and Red Sam said it was no use talking about it, she was exactly right. The children ran outside into the white sunlight and looked at the monkey in the lacy chinaberry tree. *He was busy catching fleas on himself and biting each one carefully between his teeth as if it were a delicacy.*[italics added]

Nevertheless, the initial impression of the episodic and the directionless is functional in the story. When the grandmother notes the mileage on the car—she "wrote this down because she thought it would be interesting to say how many miles they had been when they got back"—she reveals the family's trip as mere empty movement through space. Only with the accident that ends the outer journey does the action take on coherence and direction. Now the true, inner journey begins, and its destination is not Florida but death. Exterior motion in the second half of the story is minimal; aside from the eloquently understated trips into the woods, all physical traveling is over. The characters are now so motionless that small gestures acquire a disproportionate expressiveness, and the focus shifts from actions to words, from the episodic movement toward Florida to the gradually unfolding dialogue between the grandmother and The Misfit.

That dialogue has a continuity and cumulative force that is precisely what the action of the first half of the story lacked. Through it O'Connor achieves the mutual unmasking of these central figures, a process necessarily different for each, but nonetheless parallel and wrought out of their mutual interaction. If the action of the first half of the story is that of random exterior movement, that of the second is a progressive motion toward the deepest interiors of these two characters. Both figures are subjected to the distinctive O'Connor pressure, that intensity of situation that strips away the accretions of the false self.

This gradual revelation is most evident in The Misfit; indeed, if we fail to recognize the progression in his unburdening, he will seem simply inconsistent. At first, for all the menace in his appearance, The Misfit is remarkably well-mannered toward his intended victims. He blushes at Bailey's "shocking" remark to the old woman, consoles her, apologizes for his half-dressed condition "before you ladies" and couches his murderous orders in a deferential gentility: "Would you mind stepping back in them woods . . ." But the grandmother's desperate flattery gradually moves him beyond mere politeness. At first her accolade, "I know you're a good man," produces only the formulaic, "I pre-chate that, lady," but a few moments later the same remark elicits a more carefully considered response: "Nome, I ain't a good man" (p. 128). With this, The Misfit shifts to another level, gradually uncovering the dimensions of his quest to "know why it is," a quest that has led him to the tomblike penitentiary and a sense of the baffling injustice of life. But when the grandmother self-servingly introduces religion into the dialogue, she forces another turn of the screw, although again the shift is not apparent at once:

> "If you would pray," the old lady said, "Jesus would help you."
> "That's right," The Misfit said.
> "Then why don't you pray!" she asked. . . .
> "I don't want no hep," he said. "I'm doing all right by myself."

The offhand acknowledgment here of the efficacy of Jesus and the claim to self-sufficiency without Him gradually gives way to the famous passage already quoted where The Misfit confesses his doubt of Jesus and poses his stark alternatives. There The Misfit shows himself as literally a rational animal, reasoning with a frighteningly icy logic to arrive at a snarl like that of the family cat as he speaks his doctrine of Jesus or meanness. But there is a still deeper self beyond that. Pretensions to "doing all right by myself" drop away, and what appears is the face of the anguished and angry child: "'It ain't right I wasn't there [when Jesus claimed to have raised the dead]. . . . Listen lady,' he said in a high voice, 'if I had of been there I would of known and I wouldn't be like I am now.'" The center has at last been reached, and the painful uncertainty there is only confirmed by his (and the story's) final line: "It's no real pleasure in life."

The revelation of The Misfit is a gradual one, the piercing through of layer after layer until we arrive at the core of his torment. The unmasking of the grandmother follows a different curve, the rising intensity of her habitual responses, which, reaching the point of hysteria, suddenly burst like a bubble; and out of the wreckage emerges a more deeply authentic self. Her situation, at least, is symbolized by the relative physical postures of the two antagonists. Whereas The Misfit "squats" soon after his entrance into the story and does not budge from that position until he leaps back to shoot the old woman, the grandmother stands "looking down on him" through almost all of their dialogue. She begins with her genteel flattery—"I know you're a good man . . . . I know you must come from nice people!" [the line that had recently worked so well with Red Sammy]—proceeds through advice for gaining middle-class security ("Think how wonderful it would be to settle down and live a comfortable life"), and, all else failing, grasps frantically at her religiosity. Nothing silences the gunshots from the woods, and the grandmother's final attempt to stave off the inevitable is a hysterically garbled parody of all her arguments: "'Jesus!' the old lady cried. 'You've got good blood! I know you wouldn't shoot a lady! I know you come from nice people! Pray! Jesus, you ought not to shoot a lady. I'll give you all the money I've got!'"

There is nowhere further to go in that direction, and amongst the shattered confusion of her customary values, she collapses from her position above The Misfit, literally sinking down to his level of anguish and uncertainty. She cannot answer his arguments, but, stripped of her middle-class pretensions and self-serving assurances, she can, and does, respond as a "grand-mother" (and she is given no other name) to his suffering. Rather than attempting to manipulate those around her to her own ends, for the first time she "reach[es]" out to the need of this surrogate child. The Misfit, of course, shoots her at once. The mutual revelations thus come together: as he discloses his deepest torment, she responds with her deepest self. It is the convergence that the entire latter half of "A Good Man Is Hard to Find" has been moving relentlessly toward.

If the action of the two parts of the story is remarkably different both in kind and direction, O'Connor's control of narrative voice and tone works toward creating a sustained aesthetic whole. The dominant tone of the first half of "A Good Man Is Hard to Find" must certainly be called comic, but it is O'Connor at her most ironically astringent and sharply satirical, and the voice that, for example, presents the children's mother—her face "as broad and innocent as a cabbage and . . . tied around with a green head-kerchief that had two points on the top like a rabbit's ears" (p. 117) is ruthlessly detached from her characters. The very chilliness of the comic distance here might itself be felt as a bit unnerving. Moreover, there is a darkly menacing undertone that runs throughout the first part of the story in the form of recurrent references to violence and death: the various allusions to the exploits of The Misfit which, more than foreshadowing his later appearance, suggest the inability of the characters genuinely to imagine what he represents; the grandmother's complacent fantasizing of her own violent death in a car accident or of her cat asphyxiating himself; the graveyard that is the occasion for an arch joke; the violence of those dreadful children toward each other and their father; the verbal aggressiveness of Red Sammy's wife; even the name of the town Toombsboro.

This sinister undertone moves closer to the surface when the family turns off the main road—"The dirt road was hilly and there were sudden washes in it and sharp curves on dangerous embankments"—and deepens still further when the hidden cat springs "with a snarl" to precipitate the accident. With the threateningly slow appearance of The Misfit and his accomplices in the "hearse-like automobile," it spreads into the central action of the story, which it will dominate until the end.

As the menacing undercurrent of the first part of the story rises to dominate the second, the prevailing comedy of the first half sinks and darkens still further, but it does not disappear. The elaborate politeness of The Misfit has already been mentioned; in the midst of the ruthless death dealing, it repeatedly strikes a bizarrely incongruous note. Consider the exchange about The Misfit's improper attire which comes just after Bailey and his son have been escorted into the woods:

> "I'm sorry I don't have a shirt on before you ladies," he said, hunching his shoulders slightly. "We buried our clothes that we had on when we escaped and we're just making do until we can get better. We borrowed these from some folks we met," he explained.
>
> "That's perfectly all right," the grandmother said. "Maybe Bailey has an extra shirt in his suitcase."
>
> "I'll look and see terrectly," The Misfit said.

It is all very well bred, but since the story has begun with the grandmother admonishing her son to "read here what it says [The Misfit] did to these people," the context and the euphemistic *borrowed* makes the entire exchange horrifyingly ludicrous—black comedy indeed. And here as elsewhere the grandmother becomes not less but more absurd, for her sentimental gentilities were never so preposterously at odds with the actual situation.

The extension of comic perception throughout the sinister second part of the story is a reminder that the coolly observant narrator, the detached voice of the first part, is still present, noting the terrors of this family, and especially of the grandmother, from the same emotional distance that she reported their follies. When the grandmother first recognizes The Misfit, this passage occurs: "'You wouldn't shoot a lady, would you?' the grandmother said and removed a clean handkerchief from her cuff and began to slap at her eyes with it". The old lady has just learned that she faces almost certain death and she is understandably frightened, but the precise notation of action and the single word *slap* preserve the narrative distance: no sympathy is added to her self-pity here. When the last of five pistol shots sounds from the woods, "the grandmother raised her head like a parched old turkey hen crying for water and called, 'Bailey Boy, Bailey Boy!'" (p. 132). Those pistol reports signify the end of her entire family, but the animal simile qualifies and contains the pathos inherent in the situation. The controlled detachment of the narrative voice perhaps makes the horror of the second half of the story bearable, but such unflappable poise is more than a little frightening in itself. In any case, the sustained consistency of that voice is a powerful means of binding the two sections of the story together.

O'Connor's use of tone and voice thus works toward reconciling the two halves of "A Good Man Is Hard to Find" despite the rather disparate action contained in each. Tonally the story maintains a mixture of the comic and the sinister throughout, with different emphases as demanded by the differing kinds of action, and the narrative voice preserves its ironic detachment with implacable consistency. More, however, remains to be said about precisely that incident which seems to snap the action of the story in two, the car accident, for of course that event is by no means as simple as I have suggested above.

If O'Connor at first glance appears to insist on the melodrama of the car's overturn by having the children underline it with their delighted screams, "A Good Man Is Hard to Find" does not allow the attentive reader to miss the sense in which that accident is not accidental at all, but the responsibility of the grandmother. We recall the story's opening in which, wanting to travel to Tennessee rather than Florida, she attempts to change the family's mind by a hypocritical use of the threat of The Misfit, and we particularly savor the irony of "I wouldn't take my children in any direction with a criminal like that aloose in it. I couldn't answer to my conscience if I did". For this of course is exactly what she does. The detour that leads to that accident on a deserted dirt road is a response to her nostalgia for an antebellum mansion where, she fibs enticingly, legend holds that treasure is hidden—a house, she belatedly remembers (and again we note the irony), which is not in Georgia at all, but in Tennessee. The immediate cause of the accident is the cat she has smuggled along against her son's wishes "because he would miss her too much and she was afraid he might brush against one of the gas burners and accidentally asphyxiate himself." In all of this we recognize how the grandmother's rampant selfishness, her sentimentality, gentility, nostalgia, materialism, and uncertain hold on reality have contributed to the accident on this sinister back road. The ironies, up to this point in the story, are evident and a bit pat.

But through The Misfit the second half of "A Good Man Is Hard to Find" raises questions at another level altogether and invites a reevaluation of the import of the car accident. The first imbalance in the world that he had detected was not that introduced by Jesus. This prior one he articulates in explaining his act of self-naming:

> "I call myself The Misfit," he said, "because I can't make what all I done wrong fit with what all I gone through in punishment."
>
> There was a piercing scream from the woods, followed closely by a pistol report. "Does it seem right to you, lady, that one is punished a heap and another ain't punished at all?"

Again, we note the irony of the juxtaposition (although, given the premises The Misfit gradually reveals, the logic of his "mean" actions is frighteningly consistent), but the problem of justice he raises here bears directly on the upshot of the car accident. By any human standards, does it seem "right" that not only the grandmother herself but her entire family down to the baby should be murderously "punished" for "what all [she] done wrong"? Even if we grant that the old lady bears responsibility for the accident, is she also responsible for the fact that this dirt road, of all the dirt roads in Georgia, is the one that harbors The Misfit and his gang? In light of the consequences of the car wreck, that accident is, in a deeper sense, fully as melodramatic as it first appeared.

The form of "A Good Man Is Hard to Find" thus supports The Misfit's arguments, for to him life *is* melodrama: if he says his punishment exceeds his crimes, the two parts of the story show both this family's sins and the excessiveness of their punishment. Thus far, however, The Misfit has been considering the problem of suffering horizontally, as it were, finding it unresolvable by human reason, unamenable to the desire to make this world fit into coherent patterns. It is only now that he introduces the other possibility, the vertical dimension of another life through which such dilemmas might be resolved. Unlike the problem of justice horizontally considered, this question requires not the mental weighing of experiences, but the fullest commitment of the self—thus the off-balance demand which it forces. The choice is finally a stark either/or, which to The Misfit takes the form of Jesus or meanness.

O'Connor's own remarks on this story (and everywhere else) leave of course no doubt where she felt herself committed. Emphasizing the grandmother's recognition of The Misfit and calling it her "moment of grace," she insisted that the assumptions underlying her writing were those of "the central Christian mysteries" (*Mystery and Manners* 112, 109). And it would seem difficult, watching the grandmother reach out to The Misfit as "one of [her] own babies" or responding to the overtones of her final posture ("her legs crossed under her like a child's and her face smiling up at the cloudless sky"), seriously to dispute this element in the story. Nevertheless, however childlike or smiling, that final posture does belong to a corpse, the object not only of the acknowledged meanness of The Misfit, but of a more devious cruelty in the story.

O'Connor was once approached directly on the question of the tension in her work: "If the Redemption is a framework for your writing, how do you account for the brutality in your stories?" In reply, she cited "A Good Man Is Hard to Find": "There really isn't much brutality. . . . People keep referring to the brutality in the stories, but even 'A Good Man Is Hard to Find' is, in a way, a comic stylized thing. It is not naturalistic writing and so you can't really call it brutal." Apparently taking *brutality* here to mean simply violent action, O'Connor's response, perhaps deliberately, evades the question, implying that one can speak of cruelty only in connection with identifiably naturalistic writing (recall her admonition to ignore "the dead bodies" in "A Good Man Is Hard to Find"!). Most interesting of all is her failure (or refusal) to recognize that the comic, far from automatically ruling out cruelty, may itself be simply a more subtle source of it.

As O'Connor herself seems here to acknowledge, "A Good Man Is Hard to Find" may well be her most violent story, but it is also one in which the comic tone is at its most astringent, the ironic voice at its most drily mocking. The first half of the story is given over to the narrator's relentless revelation of the selfishness, the vacuousness, the nastiness of this family, and especially of its key member, the grandmother. In the exposure of her smugness, pretentiousness, and hypocrisy, of her egoistic manipulation of others, of the role of all these qualities in the causing of the car accident, the presentation walks a fine tonal line between laughter and outrage. The manner of her portrayal in the opening part of the story creates the expectation that the sequel will provide her with some comeuppance, that she will be made to offer satisfaction for such behavior. If, as I have argued above, the punishment that does come seems by all reasonable standards excessive, nevertheless the sense of satisfaction is projected into the landscape of the story, for as the murderous gunshots begin to echo from the woods, the very sound of the wind in the trees becomes "like a long satisfied insuck of breath" (p. 129). It might indeed be argued that the violence of the second part of "A Good Man Is Hard to Find" is the transposition of the biting tone of the first onto the level of action. In any case, the climax of the story manages to have it both ways at once. The grandmother does indeed have what O'Connor calls her "special kind of triumph," her "moment of grace," but she is made to pay immediately not only for that moment but for all her conduct with her life. At this point the two poles of The Misfit's conundrum, Jesus and meanness, converge, and the ambivalence is captured in the final image of the grandmother as a beatific corpse in a puddle of blood.

The full resonance of The Misfit's shooting depends upon our recollection of the grandmother's position in her family, for "A Good Man" is among the first of O'Connor's mature stories to revolve around the conflict between generations. The old lady's recognition of this criminal as "one of my own children" is made literally plausible by his donning of the same shirt her son Bailey had been wearing earlier, but in the imaginative economy of the story that shirt signifies the symbolic presence of the now-dead son through the rest of The Misfit's confrontation with the grandmother. Bailey's most salient trait, his edgy sullenness, is clearly the mask of suppressed anger toward his garrulous and manipulative mother, an anger that bursts through only once, in his "shocking" rebuke to her when she identifies The Misfit. That psychopath has of course his own reasons for shooting her, but when he does so he also symbolically acts out the rage that Bailey has smothered, the repayment of all her crafty domineering and self-serving hypocrisy, for the smuggled cat, the dirt road, the car accident, the blurting out of the name that ensures the family's doom. It is the first, but not the last, occasion in O'Connor's fiction when the confrontation between a mother and an angry child results in violent death.

The encounter between the grandmother and The Misfit that occupies the second half of "A Good Man" is thus in one sense an extension and deepening of the more sporadic and superficial battle between the old lady and her family in the first half. Punctuated by the gunshots from the woods, their confrontation is also the most obvious source of the tensions within the story, and O'Connor uses the juxtaposition of this strangely mismatched pair to introduce those thematic misfits of crime and punishment, Jesus and meanness, and further echoes these dualities in a structure which divides the action midway with the car accident. Aesthetically, as we have seen, the story is sustained by the persistence of the coolly detached narrative voice throughout and by the careful control of comic and sinister tonal elements in both parts of the work. Nevertheless, O'Connor's use of melodramatic action is nowhere clearer than in "A Good Man Is Hard to Find," the tensions between violent material and comic treatment nowhere more blatantly exploited. At the climax of the story, we receive rapid successive glimpses of both the grandmother's soul and her dead body, an intimation of Jesus and an expression of meanness, the antithetical terms momentarily brought together in the image of her smiling corpse. It is a paradoxical joining, but without these poles "A Good Man Is Hard to Find" would not exist at all.

MICHAEL O. BELLAMY

Everything Off Balance:
Protestant Election in
Flannery O'Connor's
"A Good Man Is Hard to Find"

Robert Milder's article, "The Protestantism of Flannery O'Connor," is based on two essential aspects of Protestantism he finds in O'Connor's so-called Catholic fiction: "The first is an insistence upon the absolute and irremediable corruption of the natural man, and consequently upon the necessity of divine grace for every good work; the second is an exaltation of private religious experience at the expense of the sacraments and the institutional Church." Late in his essay, Milder mentions that "A Good Man Is Hard to Find" is one of O'Connor's more Catholic stories.[1] I would like to take issue with Milder, not because of his association of O'Connor's writings with Protestantism, but rather because, at least in the case of "A Good Man," he does not go far enough. It is difficult to explain the crucial event in this story, the sudden and abrupt conversion of the grandmother, without reference to evangelical Protestantism. Moreover, The Misfit, the other major character in "A Good Man," is a visible manifestation of the theological contradictions which Milder describes in his discussion of O'Connor: much like his author, The Misfit is a Bible Belt Fundamentalist in spite of himself. Thus, we can learn something significant about this story in particular, as well as its author's more generally significant religious beliefs, by considering the extent to which "A Good Man" reveals the conflict between Flannery O'Connor's avowed Catholicism and her tendency to view religious experience in the context of Protestant Election.

On the most general level, the story has resonances of the typical spiritual allegory of the Protestant pilgrim. Once this overall similarity to the situation in, say, *Pilgrim's Progress,* is established, specific differences stand forth. The family in O'Connor's story is on a journey, but unlike the pilgrim in Bunyan's book, they are literally, and spiritually, on vacation; it is appropriate that they get lost, for, though they are headed for Florida in a sense, they are really going nowhere. O'Connor's story also differs from Bunyan's in that the entire family comes along; given the incessant bickering of the family in "A Good Man Is Hard to Find," it is obvious, in retrospect, why the pilgrim in *Pilgrim's Progress* who hopes to succeed must leave his family behind. The accident that ends with the automobile "in a gulch off the side of the road"[2] is reminiscent of the "slough of despond" that temporarily interrupts the quest in *Pilgrim's Progress.* The crucial difference is that the family does not survive. Their executor, The Misfit, appears on the road above them in his "hearse-like" automobile, an Anti-Christ in his chariot, announcing the apocalypse. The Misfit's role as an Anti-Christ is subsequently maintained by other ironic inversions of divine characteristics. Unlike Christ, who suffered little children to come unto Him, The Misfit shuns John Wesley and June Star, for children make him "nervous." His reference to the fact that he "was a different sort of dog" from his brothers and sisters is similarly indicative of his satanic nature, for "dog" is, of course "God" spelled backwards, and demonology is based on inverting the sacred.

This set of inversions is consistent with The Misfit's entire personality, for he is a sort of Protestant exegetical scholar *manqué.* Temperamentally, he is suited for the kind of profound, sustained curiosity that motivates the biblical scholar. His father used to describe this trait in a down-to-earth way: "It's some that can live their whole life out without asking about it and it's others has to know why it is, and this boy is one of the latters. He's going to be into everything." The Misfit even looks like a scholar: "His hair was just beginning to gray and he wore silver-rimmed spectacles that gave him a scholarly look." Like many literal interpreters of the Bible, he has an inordinate respect for the written word. He does not, for example, question that he is guilty of the crime for which he was originally sent to prison, though he confesses he cannot recall exactly what he did. But never mind, he tells the grandmother: "It wasn't no mistake. They had the papers on me." For the original, but impossible, goal of tracking down his original sin, he has substituted the rectitude of keeping good records:

> He [Jesus] hadn't committed any crime and they could prove I had committed one because they had the papers on me. That's why I sign myself

now. I said long ago, you can get a signature and sign everything you do and keep a copy of it. Then you'll know what you done and you can hold up the crime to the punishment and see do they match and in the end you'll have something to prove you ain't been treated right.

His interpretation of the prison psychiatrist's oedipal diagnosis is similarly indicative of exaggerated faith in the literal word. His literal understanding of Freud is but a secular correlative of a Fundamentalist reading of the Bible:

It was a head-doctor at the penitentiary said what I had done was kill my daddy but I known that for a lie. My daddy died in nineteen ought nineteen of the epidemic flu and I never had a thing to do with it. He was buried in the Mount Hopewell Baptist churchyard and you can go there and see for yourself.

The Misfit is the man from Missouri who believes only in what he has seen; thus we learn immediately the difference between the grandmother's hypocrisy and his fidelity to his own experience when he corrects her version of the accident, stating that the car actually only turned over "Oncet," for he had seen it happen. All he lacks is faith, for had he been there when Jesus "raised the dead," he would have immediately and radically changed his life:

Jesus was the only One that ever raised the dead . . . and He shouldn't have done it. He thown everything off balance. If He did what He said, then it's nothing for you to do but thow away everything and follow Him, and if He didn't, then it's nothing for you to do but enjoy the few minutes you got left the best way you can—by killing somebody or burning down his house or doing some other meanness to him. No pleasure but meanness.

The central message of The Misfit's sermon, for a sermon is what his remarks amount to, is a familiar one in Flannery O'Connor's fiction; there is no middle ground between absolute belief in Christ's messianic function and a belief that life is nasty, brutish, and short. In fact, since The Misfit lacks faith in Christ's resurrection, he actually sees it as his duty to make life nastier, shorter, and more brutish. Implicit in the Manichean reduction of life to two antithetical alternatives is the Protestant insistence on man's total depravity without God's saving grace. The Misfit describes this belief as it applies to himself: "I found out the crime don't matter. You can do one thing or you can do another, kill a man or take a tire off his car, because sooner or later you're going to forget what it was you done and just be punished for it." The Misfit not only assumes that man is inherently guilty; he also assumes men are individually responsible for Original Sin. Given this congenital depravity, man is utterly incapable of doing anything to effect his own salvation. To do so would be roughly equivalent to pulling himself up by his own bootstraps. Here we have the surest sign of Protestantism: the absolute necessity of faith and, as a corollary, the belief that good works are at most merely a sign of God's favor.

The Misfit must be given credit for acting in conformity with his nature. We cannot say as much for the grandmother, for she is, until the moment of her death, a thorough hypocrite. It is of crucial importance that her election occurs at the very moment when she is at her most hypocritical. She has, in fact, just conceded—she will do anything to survive—that "maybe He [Christ] didn't raise the dead" after all. The moment of her election merits quoting at length:

> "Maybe He didn't raise the dead," the old lady mumbled, not knowing what she was saying and feeling so dizzy that she sank down in the ditch with her legs twisted under her. . . .
>
> "I wasn't there so I can't say He didn't," The Misfit said. "I wisht I had of been there," he said, hitting the ground with his fist. "It ain't right I wasn't there because if I had of been there I would of known. Listen, lady," he said in a high voice, "if I had of been there I would of known and I wouldn't be like I am now." His voice seemed about to crack and the grandmother's head cleared for an instant. She saw the man's face twisted close to her own as if he were going to cry and she murmured, "Why you're one of my babies. You're one of my own children!" She reached out and touched him on the shoulder. The Misfit sprang back as if a snake had bitten him and shot her three times through the chest. Then he put his gun down on the ground and took off his glasses and began to clean them.
>
> Hiram and Bobby Lee returned from the woods and stood over the ditch, looking down at the grandmother who half sat and half lay in a puddle of blood with her legs crossed under her like a child's and her face smiling up at the cloudless sky.

It is clear that the grandmother is a better woman at the moment of her death than she had been at any time heretofore; or, as The Misfit puts it, "She would of been a good woman if it had been somebody there to shoot her every minute of her life." The grandmother's salvation occurs when "her head cleared for an instant"; thus her legs, earlier described as "twisted" under her, are, subsequent to her salvation, "crossed under her like a child's." Similarly, for the first and only time, she imitates the rhetoric of the New Testament, not for her own selfish purposes, but because she actually feels a maternal concern for The Misfit as one of her own children.

The extraordinary thing about the grandmother's story is the radical discontinuity between her behavior and her redemption. In fact, this discontinuity is most apparent during the moments that immediately precede her conversion. How could the irrelevance of good works for salvation be more effectively demonstrated? How could there be any relationship between good works and election when it is the confrontation with death that brings about the moment of grace? Clearly, the grandmother will not be around for any good works, since her death is the occasion for her conversion.

There is another more explicit indication of the paradoxical relationship between merit and outcome in "A Good Man": The Misfit's very name is itself indicative of his inability to discover how his punishment fits his crime. This discontinuity is but the converse of the discrepancy between the grandmother's behavior and her extraordinary fate. If Christ has, in fact, "thown everything off balance" by overcoming death, His offer of salvation through grace has also disturbed the balance of the scales of justice. Again, broadly speaking, the imbalance implicit in the irrelevance of good works and the emphasis on the gift of faith [is] Protestant. The Misfit accepts this imbalance as the only conceivable interpretation of Christianity, even as he agonizes over the injustice of his own damnation. For without the gift of faith, The Misfit is inevitably unable to establish whether or not Christ actually rose from the dead: "It ain't right I wasn't there because if I had of been there I would of known. Listen, Lady ... if I had of been there I would of known and I wouldn't be like I am now." Where, he asks, is the justice in a world in which grace is a gift, a gift he feels temperamentally incapable of receiving? Where is justice when the word "grace" actually means "favor"? For surely, by the very definition of the word, some people are "favored" or "gifted" and some are not.

This radical discontinuity between man's efforts and the divine gift of grace is the most obvious, and the most important, aspect of Flannery O'Connor's Protestantism. Again, the discontinuity is apparent in fates of both of the main characters in "A Good Man": The Misfit is genuinely concerned—in fact he is obsessed—with the ultimate issues of the human condition, while the grandmother, up to the very instant of her election, is a nauseating hypocrite. Thus, The Misfit's sincere efforts to investigate his place in the universe are to no avail, while the grandmother seems to stumble into salvation. Milder's comments on Protestantism are illuminating with respect to the fate of both characters. The attempt of The Misfit to understand his condition is bound to fail, for total depravity decrees "that man's reason has become so obscured since the Fall and his nature so debased that he is wholly incapable of virtue in his unregenerate state"

(Milder 807). On the other hand, Milder's remarks on the grandmother are revealing to the extent that they tend to distort her experience. He sees "A Good Man" as one of O'Connor's more Catholic works in that the grandmother's election demonstrates "a free acceptance of grace," an aspect of the episode that Milder sees as "one of the few remaining doctrinal points which . . . [links Flannery O'Connor] to the Catholic tradition" (817). In the first place, it is obvious that "acceptance," free or otherwise, is not a very active word to describe the grandmother's role in the episode. Even at that, her will is barely apparent in what looks like a gratuitous gesture that is utterly antithetical to everything else in her life. In fact, her attempt to touch The Misfit is much like the existentialists' gratuitous act in its radical discontinuity from what went before. Given the doctrine of total depravity, election must be gratuitous, which is to say a gift given out of the context of the receiver's life. Thus, the grandmother is suddenly converted by an overwhelming infusion of grace, an experience much like St. Paul's abrupt enlightenment at the moment of his fall from his horse. What we have, in short, is Protestant election.

There are obvious aesthetic advantages to this kind of abrupt turnabout through a direct confrontation with God. The experience of election, as Milder perceptively points out, is far more likely to be dramatically moving than gradual spiritual improvement through the mediation of the sacraments or the practice of good works. But what is missing from the stunning conversion of the grandmother is the sense of balance, the sense of justice, so central to what Thomas Aquinas called the *via media*, or the middle way.[3] Acting in good faith is not, in this context, acting according to a specific body of doctrine, but rather the sort of endeavor The Misfit describes. He feels this kind of effort ought to be sufficient, but he does not believe it actually is. Conversely, the world in which the grandmother seems to be so arbitrarily saved, so far off the beaten track, or what we might call a middle way, does seem off-balance. The grotesque element that so many people have noted in O'Connor's fiction is in great part a result of this puzzling void between the few who seem to be somewhat arbitrarily saved, and just about everybody else, the depraved. This void is also a major feature of the surrealistic element in O'Connor's fiction, the nightmarish quality that pervades the allegorical landscapes in which her grotesque figures engage in Manichean struggle. But if we step back from the works and view them in the context of their author's avowed beliefs, the most significant struggle is not this Manichean battle between good and evil, but rather the conflict between Flannery O'Connor's tendency to conceive of the human condition in terms of stark polarities, and the tendency, infrequently fulfilled but implicit in her Catholicism, to view mankind in the context of a middle way. It is because of this second attitude that the world of her fiction appears to The Misfit, to the Catholic humanist in Flannery O'Connor, and no doubt to many readers as well, as off-balance, almost at times in fact, as grotesque.

NOTES

[1] Robert Milder, "The Protestantism of Flannery O'Connor," *The Southern Review*, 11 (1975), 802–19. The quote about Protestantism is on page 806; the reference to "A Good Man Is Hard to Find" is on page 817.

[2] Flannery O'Connor, *A Good Man Is Hard to Find and Other Stories* (New York: Harcourt, 1955), p. 19. Subsequent quotations are from this edition.

[3] In fact, Milder also mentions this fundamental difference between Catholicism and Evangelical Protestantism (806–07).

HALLMAN B. BRYANT

Reading the Map in "A Good Man Is Hard to Find"

Flannery O'Connor, remarking on her most famous short story, "A Good Man Is Hard to Find," issues several caveats to critics. She allows that "a certain amount of what is the significance of this" kind of investigation has to go on in teaching and in literary analysis, but she cautions against reducing a story to "a problem to be solved" so that it becomes "something which you evaporate to get Instant Enlightenment."

Without evaporating too much I will try to shed light on the significance of some small details in "A Good Man Is Hard to Find." Although I do not think an analysis of O'Connor's use of place names in the story will create instant enlightenment, I believe that the towns alluded to along the route which the family travels were chosen for two reasons: first, and most obviously, to foreshadow; and second, to augment the theme of the story. Furthermore, because the numerous places mentioned in the story can actually be found on the map, with only one important exception, it is thus possible to estimate within a few miles the physical distance that the family travels.

The first thing one notices about "A Good Man Is Hard to Find" is that it is set in a real place—in the state of Georgia. The opening scene describes an Atlanta family quarreling about their vacation plans. The grandmother is opposed to going to Florida ostensibly because a convict "that calls himself The Misfit is aloose from the Federal pen and headed toward Florida." (Apparently the Federal penitentiary from which The Misfit has escaped is the one in Atlanta, although it is not specified in the story.) Regardless of the threat posed by The Misfit, the family heads south for Florida instead of east Tennessee where the grandmother had tried to persuade them to take her. We are told that the family left Atlanta at 8:35 in the morning with the mileage on the car at 55890, a fact recorded by the grandmother because she "thought it would be interesting to say how many miles they had been when they got back." From this point on one can literally follow the journey of the family with a road map and take the mileage they put on their car before the wreck and the subsequent meeting with The Misfit and his henchmen.

One odd fact about their route emerges immediately to anyone familiar with Atlanta and its environs. Although the family lives in Atlanta and is headed south, we are told that they pass Stone Mountain along the way. This natural phenomenon and tourist attraction is about fifteen or sixteen miles from Atlanta on the northeast side of the city. At the time the story was written, one had to follow U.S. 78 North to get to Stone Mountain, a highly unlikely road to take out of Atlanta if one is going to Florida.[1]

Although one of the children urges his father to "go through Georgia fast so we won't have to look at it much," there nevertheless are some interesting details of scenery along the roadside, and the grandmother tells us about many of the things they pass by. She notices "a cute little pickaninny" standing in the door of a shanty that she fancies would make a nice study for a sentimental painting, but the same subject disgusts her granddaughter June Star, who comments acidly, "He didn't have any britches on." More significantly, the grandmother points out a graveyard with five or six graves fenced off in the middle of a large cotton field, which is a rather obvious foreshadowing of the fate that will befall the family.

When the grandmother can no longer hold the children's attention with roadside attractions, she tells them a story of one of her girlhood suitors, Mr. Edgar Atkins Teagarden, who was from Jasper, Georgia, a small north Georgia town located in Pickens County and approximately fifty or sixty miles from the Tennessee state line. Although we are not told just where the grandmother is from, only that she has "connections in east Tennessee," it seems that to be consistent with her tale of Mr. Teagarden's courtship, she would have to have lived somewhere near Jasper, since he drove to her house by buggy every Saturday and gave her a watermelon monogrammed with his initials, E. A. T.

The family's journey is interrupted by a stop for a lunch of barbecued sandwiches at a café called The Tower which is located in "a clearing outside of Timothy." For economic effect this is one of the great scenes in all of Flannery O'Connor's fiction; yet here one cannot plot the location of the place on the map for there is no town of Timothy in Georgia. (If there is, it is such a small community it is not listed in the state atlas.) Since the other references to places in the story are to actual localities in the state, why does she create a fictitious name at this point? My theory is that in this scene, which has strong moral intention, O'Connor select[s] the name Timothy for the ironic effect it would produce. The allusion here is not geographical but Biblical, and the Timothy alluded to is almost certainly the book in the New Testament which bears the same name. Usually referred to as the Pastoral Letters, this gospel purports to be letters from Paul addressed to his disciples and through them to the Christian community at large. More than any other writing in the New Testament, the letters to Timothy are concerned with Christian orthodoxy. In this gospel Paul deals essentially with three topics: the opposition of false doctrine; the organization of the church and establishment of ecclesiastical regulations; and exhortations which indicate how to be a good citizen and Christian.

It seems to me that the concerns expressed by Paul in his letter to Timothy are very germane to the concerns expressed by Flannery O'Connor in "A Good Man Is Hard to Find," especially the concern with heretics and the advice on how to be a good Christian. One has only to set the family of six from Atlanta and Red Sammy and his wife (as well as The Misfit)—all of whom Flannery O'Connor considers heretics—against certain passages from Timothy to see that O'Connor's allusion ironically tells us just where these modern-day people are in error. For example, these verses seem to apply especially to Bailey. "He [the husband] must manage his own family well and see that his children obey him with proper respect" (I Tim. 3:4–5).

Also the author of the epistle commands good Christians to keep the faith and avoid "vain discussions" and concern with trivial matters and endless wrangling about genealogies (I Tim. 6:3–10). Further, he admonishes women "to dress modestly, with decency and propriety" and "to learn in quietness and full submission . . . and be silent" (I Tim. 2:9–12). This instruction seems to bear most directly on the grandmother, who is vain about her Old South heritage and certainly conscious of her social standing and what is required to be a lady. This is best brought out in her selection of attire for the trip. She is turned out in white gloves, black purse, a navy blue straw sailor hat with white violets on the brim, a navy blue polka dot dress with collar and cuffs of white organdy trimmed with lace, and on her neck she has pinned a purple spray of cloth violets containing a sachet. Her costume has been prepared so that, in the event of an accident, "anyone seeing her dead on the highway would know at once that she was a lady."

The grandmother's superficial conception of values is ironically underscored in the vain discussions with her grandchildren about what kind of conduct was once expected from children and her trivial remarks about plantation days and old suitors. Nowhere are her ideas more tellingly satirized than in her conversation with Red Sammy in the café where both complain of misplaced trust in their fellow man, which the grandmother sees as an indication of the general lack of manners in the modern world. She tells Red Sammy, "People are certainly not nice like they used to be." Of course, both Red Sammy and the grandmother are conceited enough to think that they are just as good as they ought to be. When Red Sammy complains of a recent theft of some gasoline by men driving a Chrysler and asks in a puzzled way why he had trusted them, he is quickly told by the grandmother that it was "because you're a good man," to which he candidly assents, "Yes'm, I suppose so."

The grandmother's inability to "learn in quietness" is tragically the cause of the deaths of the entire family. Shortly after Bailey overturns the car in a ditch, they are approached by a bespectacled man who the grandmother feels is "someone she knew" and soon she recognizes the stranger as The Misfit whose picture she has seen, and she blurts out this fact, saying, "You're The Misfit . . . I recognized you at once," to which he replies, "but it would have been better for all of you, lady, if you hadn't of reckernized me."

It is generally agreed that in the traumatic moments that follow in which the grandmother witnesses the deaths of her family and anticipates her own she does learn a lesson she has not heeded previously during her life. This lesson is the central message which Paul attempts to convey to Christians through Timothy and that is, "There is one God and one mediator between God and men, the Lord Jesus Christ, who gave himself to save mankind" (I Tim. 2:5). The evidence for assuming that she has come to a belated awareness that her faith has been misplaced in the pursuit of social graces and a concern with manners is limited to The Misfit's remark, "She would of been a good woman . . . if it had been somebody there to shoot her every minute of her life." Furthermore, in death she appears like a child, and her face is "smiling up at the cloudless sky," suggesting that she has found grace at last.

Another passage from Timothy seems especially applicable at this point: "The Spirit clearly says that in later times some will abandon the faith and follow deceiving spirits and things taught by demons. Such teachings come through hypocritical liars, whose consciences have been seared as with hot iron" (I Tim. 4:1–12). Although the whole cast of characters in the story has abandoned the faith and followed the wrong paths, the indictment of these lines would apply most forcibly to The Misfit who wears glasses and has a scholarly look. He has indeed been taught by demons, and from the Christian point of view that O'Connor takes in "A Good Man Is Hard to Find" he is a hypocritical liar who has no faith in a moral purpose in the universe and teaches that "it's nothing for you to do but enjoy the few minutes you got left the best way you can—by killing somebody or burning down his house or doing some other meanness to him." Thus, according to the ethics of this teacher, goodness is a matter of sadistic gratification. "No pleasure but meanness," he says, indicating how completely his conscience has been seared and his vision warped by his hedonistic atheism.

The numerous ways in which the content of this book of the New Testament dovetails with the characters and the theme of "A Good Man Is Hard to Find" could not be a complete accident. It cannot be demonstrated that Flannery O'Connor conceived of the moral of her story in terms of this specific book, but she made no bones about the fact that she wrote "from the standpoint of Christian orthodoxy;"[2] and there is no doubt that Paul wrote from a similar standpoint, and his letter to Timothy has the same hortatory, moralizing tone that we find just below the surface in "A Good Man Is Hard to Find." Thus, it seems likely that she put the town of Timothy on the map because she wanted the reader to pick up the allusion and perhaps [review] the contents of the New Testament, but more probably she saw the parallel between her modern-day characters who have left the main road of Christian faith and Paul's warning to the church when he feared it was in danger off into the byways of heresy.

Just as the name of the town where the family stops for lunch is carefully chosen, so is the name of Red Sammy's café. In Christian iconography towers are ambivalent symbols, that is, they speak *in bono* or *in malo,* to use the vocabulary of medieval exegetes, and can represent either good or evil qualities. For example, the Tower of Babel is symbolic of man's pride and stands for misbegotten human enterprises. The fate of the tower and its architects shows the consequences of overconfidence in the pursuit of fanciful ideas. (Interestingly enough, Nimrod, who began the construction of the tower, was also a mighty hunter, and like Red Sammy, a keeper of wild game, if Red Sammy's monkey can be called wild.)

As well as its nugatory meaning, the tower is a traditional symbol of the Virgin Mary and is a token of her purity and powers of transformation. Mary as the "refugee of sinners" according to Catholic doctrine is appropriately represented by the tower, a place associated with safety and sanctuary.

Outside of its Christian meaning the tower in arcane lore is a portent of disaster. In the sixteenth enigma of the Tarot pack of cards, catastrophe is indicated by the image of a tower struck by lightning. Whether O'Connor knew this fact about the meaning of the tower is uncertain, but she could not have been unaware of the former implications of the tower as a symbol, versed as she was in Biblical and church lore. It is appropriate that the conceited owner of this barbecue palace should have called it The Tower; it is ironic that this tower has no capacity to transform or give refuge.

Leaving Timothy and The Tower behind, both in the Biblical and geographical sense, the family [resume] their trip and we are told that just beyond Toombsboro, Georgia, the grandmother awakens from a nap with the recollection, mistaken as it turns out, that there is an old plantation nearby which she had visited as a girl; she even thinks she remembers the road to take to get there and tells Bailey, "It's not far from here, I know. . . . It wouldn't take over twenty minutes." As it so happens there is a Toomsboro (spelled without the "b") on the map and it is only twenty-three miles south of Milledgeville, Flannery O'Connor's home. She surely knew the place and chose to mention it because the name has an ominous ring, and it also would have been a logical terminus for the family's trip in terms of the time and distance they have traveled since leaving Atlanta in the morning. In fact, if one follows the usual route from Atlanta to Milledgeville (Georgia Highway 212), the distance is 93 miles, and if one adds to this the 23 miles further to Toomsboro, plus the estimated 15 or so miles that the detour to the plantation takes, then it can be calculated that the family has come a total of 130 miles. Considering the conditions of Georgia roads in the late 1940s, one had to drive under 50 m.p.h. to keep from knocking the wheels out of line from the numerous potholes that Governor Talmadge's highway people never patched. Thus, if one assumes that Bailey has averaged around 45 m.p.h. and takes account of the lunch stop, they have been on the road four or five hours and their meeting with The Misfit occurs in the early afternoon of a cloudless day with the mileage on the car standing at about 56020 on the meter. Sadly enough, the grandmother will be forever unaware of this "interesting fact," but we as readers should have a better understanding of how carefully O'Connor has used realistic detail for symbolic effects.

In the course of this story, the family's trip takes them from their complacent and smug living room to a confrontation with ultimate evil and ultimate reality as well. They are not prepared for the meeting because, like the heretics who concerned Paul in his epistle to Timothy, they have been occupied with the trivial things and involved in quarrels; and, like the builders of the Tower of Babel, they are preoccupied with vain enterprises.

Flannery O'Connor saw herself as a prophetic writer and her authorial strategy was to shock; her fiction is intended as a rebuke to rationalistic, materialistic and humanistic thought—the heresies of the twentieth century. She believed that people in the modern world were not following the true path and had to be made to see their condition for what it was—a wandering by the wayside. In "A Good Man Is Hard to Find" the family's wayward lives are given direction in their final moments, and from O'Connor's point of view they are at last on the right road.

NOTES

[1] The detour by Stone Mountain was probably due to O'Connor's uncertainty about its exact location; she simply found it a convenient allusion since Stone Mountain was for years Georgia's most famous tourist attraction, but perhaps there is more than meets the eye. In 1915 a project was begun by the United Daughters of the Confederacy which called for Robert E. Lee and his lieutenants to be carved in heroic scale on the vertical face of the mountain. Ironically, the artist commissioned for the job was a Yankee sculptor named Gutzon Borglum who blasted and chiseled on the mountain until 1928 when funds and patience ran out. After expenditure of hundreds of thousands of dollars in a vain effort to impose the heroes of the "Lost Cause" on the side of the mountain, the project was dropped. The scarred carvings, empty catwalks and scaffolds were reminders of a long series of errors and frustrations of the U.D.C. ladies who dreamed of keeping the past alive with a memorial that would be "the perpetuation of a vision." (See *The Story of Stone Mountain* by Willard Neal [Atlanta: Neal and Rogers, 1963], pp. 23–33). Flannery O'Connor was amused by the quixotic qualities of the U.D.C., and Stone Mountain would evoke for Georgians of O'Connor's generation the folly of a sentimental project—a project almost as futile as the grandmother's in the story, whose fascination with past grandeur is congruent with that of the U.D.C.'s and has equally unfortunate results.

[2] *The Habit of Being: Letters of Flannery O'Connor,* ed. Sally Fitzgerald (New York: Farrar, 1979), 196.

REBECCA R. BUTLER

What's So Funny About Flannery O'Connor?
(1979)

When Flannery O'Connor was asked why the story about the grisly family murder, "A Good Man Is Hard to Find," appeared to be her favorite, she corrected that impression: She chose that story for her public reading engagements, she explained, not because of a special preference for it, but because, she said, it was the only one she could get through out loud with-out laughing.[1]

Now, if any of you have ever studied or taught that particular O'Con-nor short story, you may agree with the author that it is entirely possible to read right through it without once being incapacitated by laughter. I know myself that I can keep a perfectly straight face as I read of the children and their mother being marched off into the woods at gunpoint, followed by the sounds of shots. And when the grandmother calls out to The Misfit, "'You're one of my own children!'" and he shoots her three times in the chest, I don't even smile. On the other hand, I think it would take some practice for me to maintain a deadpan throughout the grandmother's story of her youthful suitor, Mr. Edgar Atkins Teagarden from Jasper, Georgia, whose love-token, a watermelon carved with his initials, E. A. T., and left on the front porch, was eaten by an evidently literate "nigger boy." Similarly, the repartee between the grandmother and her saucy granddaughter, June Star, and the entire episode at Red Sammy Butts's barbecue house do give rise to laughter. To explain just how and why this story, which ends with the grandmother dead in a pool of her own blood, can be called comic is risky. E. B. White gives this warning to would-be analysts of comedy: "Hu-mor can be dissected," he wrote, "as a frog can, but the thing dies in the pro-cess and the innards are discouraging to any but the pure scientific mind."[2] O'Connor herself used the same image in voicing a similar complaint about the fate of her stories: "Every time a story of mine appears in a freshman anthology," she said, "I have a vision of it, with its little organs laid open, like a frog in a bottle."[3] So it seems that, as an investigator of the comic, I face two alternatives: to step aside now or to proceed with caution. I will take the second route, using as my guide Louis Rubin, himself a masterful analyst of the American comic tradition who, in his Preface to *The Comic Imagination in American Literature,* acknowledged that "writing *about* hu-mor and humorists" is necessarily "an awkward business" which always risks making the analyst look ridiculous.[4] But he went right ahead and wrote, ad-hering to the principle that understanding heightens enjoyment.

Despite O'Connor's implication that many of her stories were too funny for her to read before an audience, some critics have failed to see the humor in the O'Connor canon. In the first place, of course, some commen-tators were interested in other aspects of the work than the humorous. For a while, the words most frequently used to describe her writing belonged to one of two groups: Such words as *prophecy, vision, spiritual quest, redemptive grace, vocation,* and *sacrament* belong to one group, and to the other such words as *perverse, demonic, grotesque, insane, hostile,* and *obsessive.* In other words, most of the early criticism has emphasized the religious dimension or the psychological dimension of the work, sometimes both. An articulate appreciation of the comic dimension was slower in coming. When Martha Stephens published a study of the tone of the fiction, entitled *The Question of Flannery O'Connor*, she sparked just such an articulate assessment. In her book Stephens goes so far as to say that O'Connor was not truly a comic writer, that her novels "are not *comic novels* in any accepted sense of the term."[5] In fact, Stephens accepts only "a few stories" as belonging within the category of comedy. This thorough analysis of the fiction in terms of the deep ambivalence it seems to elicit from most readers does address intelligently some of the crucial and most complex issues of O'Connor's method, but, like so many less persuasive commentators before her, Stephens fails to maintain the double vision that O'Connor used in blending the laughable and the serious in her tales. There is an assumption, more or less obviously at work, for instance, that overt references to religion, violence, or death automatically shift the tone to the somber or horrific end of the scale. According to this same frame of reference, O'Connor's personal religious views, as they are discovered in the fiction, are so repugnant and oppressive with their contempt for ordinary human life, that they mar the entire work. As evidence of this contempt, Stephens cites the physical descriptions of characters, their ugliness, their animalistic features.

It was to this one-sided reading of such conventional comic techniques as exaggeration and caricature as indications that "human life is a sordid, almost unrelievedly hideous affair,"[6] that Carter Martin seemed to be addressing his analysis of "Comedy and Humor in Flannery O'Connor's Fiction."[7] Equally pertinent was Louis Rubin's contribution to the O'Connor Symposium in Milledgeville in 1977, "Flannery O'Connor's Company of Southerners: or, 'The Artificial Nigger' Read as Fiction Rather than Theology."[8] Martin indicates a corrective direction by reviewing the broad contours of Western comedy from Aristophanes to Jonson to Bergson; what he calls the "comic-cosmic" view of man, that more inclusive view, is certainly the one that O'Connor found most workable and is the context into which her work fits most comfortably. And, in particular, it fits into the American version of that view, as Rubin indicates by reminding us of the wealth of comic writers and characters who belong to the Middle Georgia region where Flannery attended high school and did her mature writing. Uncle Remus, Simon Suggs, Polly Peachblossom, Major Jones, Johnson Jones Hooper all lived in or hailed from this special region. And a comparison of O'Connor's comic characterizations and themes with those of Joel Chandler Harris or Augustus Baldwin Longstreet shows that, no more than they was she ridiculing, disdaining, or demeaning these poor rural folk nor their lives.

The conventions of the tradition can be understood through a meaningful perspective.

It is not unusual to be tone-deaf when encountering a new style. My own students, I know, are sometimes unable to see anything comic in Manley Pointer's theft and desertion of Joy-Hulga in "Good Country People," nor do they always laugh at Mrs. Crater's sly campaign to marry her not-entirely-eligible only daughter, Lucynell, to Mr. Shiftlet. For critics to be so unappreciative, however, is disappointing. The students, after all, know little of the stylistics of comedy, and they are only beginning to develop their imaginative "ears." For the benefit of the student or any reader new to O'Connor's fiction, a relatively brief tuning-up period is in order. First on the checklist are titles: occasionally the title will sound a bit peculiar or zany itself, like "The Artifiicial Nigger" or "You Can't Be Any Poorer Than Dead." More often the title gains comic momentum as it recurs in the story, the way "A Good Man Is Hard to Find," a familiar song title, does as it reappears as a hackneyed expression in Red Sammy Butts's conversation, and is repeated with a twist by The Misfit who, by his own admission is not a good man, but would like to be able to verify the reported goodness of Jesus. The second benchmark, applicable in any comic work, is the name of any character or place. Why name a con artist Manley Pointer, or Hoover Shoats for that matter, if your aim is a primarily sober one? And we have already mentioned Red Sammy Butts, an ideal name for a buffoon-host. Although all of O'Connor's names are actually well-known in certain Southern regions, usually they are uncommon; they seem to be chosen for their suggestiveness or their sound effect: Hooten, Parrum, Turpin, Cheatham, Godhigh, Farebrother, Ham, Block, Fox, Pitts. Place names work in a similar fashion: Taulkinham, Eastrod, Toombsboro, Timberboro, Partridge. And there are the ladies with three names, for some reason always good for a laugh: Sally Poker Sash, Lucynell Crater, Sarah Ruth Cates. In "The Displaced Person," Mrs. McIntyre's litany of worthless tenants suggests a recital of the plagues of Egypt: there were the Shortleys, Ringfields, Collinses, Garrits, Jarrells, Perkinses, Pinkins, and Herrins. From that same story, the unpronounceable Guizac is rendered "Gobblehook" by Mrs. Shortley, who also says that she'd as soon call a child Bollweevil as Sledgewig. Such films as "The Displaced Person," televised by the Public Broadcasting System as part of its American Short Story series, demonstrate a third way to overcome quickly the handicap of "wooden ear" which can strike any of us upon encountering a new writer. Because a dramatization allows us to see and hear the characters in action, the imaginative ear does not have to bear the burden of interpretation alone. Furthermore, I have seen illuminating dramatizations of "A Good Man Is Hard to Find,"

"A View of the Woods," and "Revelation." The rhythm and lilt of O'Connor's dialogue, for instance, can enter through the ear rather than be interpreted on the silent page. This can be especially important to a reader who is not native to the South. Perhaps you remember this little speech by Mr. Shortley, the dairyman whose position is threatened by a new tenant, a refugee from Poland, Mr. Guizac:

> "All men was created free and equal," he said to Mrs. McIntyre, "and I risked my life and limb to prove it. Gone over there and fought and bled and died and come back over here and find out who's got my job—just exactly who I been fighting. It was a hand-grenade come that near to killing me and I seen who throwed it—little man with eye-glasses just like his. Might have bought them at the same store. Small world," and he gave a bitter little laugh. He had the power of making other people see his logic. He talked a good deal to the Negroes.

Comic dialogue is, of course, O'Connor's specialty, and one to which we will return.

Now there's one other element of O'Connor's fiction that perhaps cannot be analyzed and explained as readily as the first three items on our checklist, but it cannot be ignored, and that is the sense of threat, of danger, of violence that, in some form, permeates all of her stories. It is a commonplace, of course, that all accomplished comedy contains or rests upon some deeply serious or horrifyingly repugnant reality. While the underlying seriousness of O'Connor's humor is relatively obvious, a simple definition will not do it justice. I am not convinced that this Southern woman, for example, was evangelizing through her fiction. I have found a comment by E. B. White on this topic that sounds so much like something she would have written that I will let it serve. White does not agree with those who say that the humorist is fundamentally a very sad person. "[I]t would be more accurate, I think," he writes, "to say that there is a deep vein of melancholy running through everyone's life and that the humorist, more sensible of it than some others, compensates for it actively and positively. Humorists fatten on trouble. They have always made trouble pay. They struggle along with a good will and endure pain cheerfully, knowing how well it will serve them in the sweet by and by."[9] And serve it does! It serves as an antidote to that mind-dulling sentimentality O'Connor attacked at every opportunity. Again and again in her occasional prose we find this word, *semtimentality*, used as a scourge against mindless Catholic readers, mindless critics, mindless writers. A similar favorite phrase was "hazy compassion," and she described one of her reader's affection for [T]he Misfit as "sentimental." In her resistance to heart-warming and uplifting characterization, O'Connor is adhering to one of comedy's oldest purposes—that of dispelling illusion. Sentimentality, as represented by the grandmother and quite a number of upright matrons, is a self-deceit that O'Connor shock tactics are designed to expose. A sentimental comedy, of course, would contain no murders, no abandonments, no strokes, no handicaps nor illnesses of a disfiguring nature. No wooden legs, no coffins too small for the body, no cans of peanut brittle filled with teeth-fracturing springs, no women pregnant in iron lungs, no wheelchair veterans left in the sun beside the Coke machine. The "paraphernalia of suffering," as Nathanael West calls it, serves as unlikely fodder for this "realist of distances," as O'Connor called herself.

Once the checklist has done its work and the newcomer is well-launched on O'Connor's comic seas, he [or she] is ready for more detailed study which could follow any of several approaches. Careful reading of a critical theorist like Northrop Frye, for instance, yields a systematic framework on which to test and measure individual stories and characters. Frye discusses the importance in Shakespearean comedy of the term "grace," a word central to O'Connor's fiction, and he explains why a religious outlook requires the comic mode. Even such a theorist as Freud, who would seem to be an unsuitable companion for O'Connor, produces a characteristically economic definition of the comical as "an unintentional discovery in social relations" that seems to match ideally with her own description of the "totally unexpected" action that serves as the pivot for each of her stories. Manley Pointer's theft of Joy-Hulga's wooden leg is just such an unexpected, unintentional discovery, not only for the reader, according to O'Connor, but for the author as well. The denouement occurred to her only lines before she wrote it! Other similar comic surprises may be profitably compared with O'Connor's from the works of Mark Twain, Eudora Welty, William Faulkner, and Nathanael West.

Consideration of the principles that unify the comic imagination in American letters should be particularly fruitful approaches to this twentieth-century Georgian. What Rubin calls "the Great American Joke" is certainly one that O'Connor was in on. America is a country that cherishes its ideals, but carefully avoids any institution that has traditionally embodied them—thus, no aristocracy, no monarchy, no state church. Ideals without institutions is the Great American Joke that allows for the triumph of the banal—from Mark Twain's Emmeline Grangerford to Nathanael West's Miss Lonelyhearts to Joseph Heller's Bob Slocum. For O'Connor, the Great American Joke paved the way for numberless religious eccentrics, probably best explored in *Wise Blood,* and for an equal number of abstracted or sentimental idealists, often her matrons, but drawn in greater detail as Rayber the pedant in *The Violent Bear It Away.* Probably more accessible for most readers is a conflict that is very much alive in virtually all American comic writing, and that is what Rubin has identified as the incompatibility of the vulgar and the genteel viewpoints within a single society. "Each persists in making the other look ridiculous," according to Rubin, "and usually that is what is funny."[10] *Huckleberry Finn* is the most widely known, extended example of this clash of cultural modes, and contains some of the most memorable examples of the language that embodies this clash, the vernacular and the refined. O'Connor fits squarely in this tradition, as her dialogue attests. Ripely vernacular, the exchanges between the landed and the servant classes, for example, demonstrate just how incompatible but how interdependent the two verbal styles are. Listen to Mrs. Hopewell, the eternal optimist, and her hired hand, Mrs. Freeman:

> When Mrs. Hopewell said to Mrs. Freeman that life was like that, Mrs. Freeman would say, "I always said so myself."
>
> She was quicker than Mr. Freeman. When Mrs. Hopewell said to her after they had been on the place a while, "You know, you're the wheel behind the wheel," and winked, Mrs. Freeman said, "I know it. I've always been quick. It's some that are quicker than others."
>
> "Everybody is different," Mrs. Hopewell said.
>
> "Yes, most people is," Mrs. Freeman said.
>
> "It takes all kinds to make the world."
>
> "I always said it did myself."
>
> The girl was used to this kind of dialogue for breakfast and more of it for dinner; sometimes they had it for supper too.

When the property-owning Mrs. Cope urges A Higher View in the story, "A Circle in the Fire," her tenant Mrs. Pritchard, parries with sour logic:

> "Every day I say a prayer of Thanksgiving. Think of all we have," she said, and sighed, "We have everything."
>
> Mrs. Pritchard studied the woods. "All I got is four abscess teeth," she remarked.

This verbal dueling is a hallmark of O'Connor's humor, and it illustrates her use of that distinctive American juxtaposition of vernacular and refined speech, each working to make the other sound laughable. Whether it takes on the tone and force of a Punch and Judy routine or the subtle shrewdness of a horse swap, every conversation in every story is essentially an argument, a contest between rival wills; and for this reason, the dialogue is a good place to take the pulse of her fiction and to discover, first, how alive, indeed, it is, and second, how completely it depends upon the tensions of unresolved opposition. Returning to the question of what place the shocking, the ugly, the violent can have in a work of comedy, in O'Connor's comedy, at least, it provides the frame, the context within which the laughable can be appreciated to full advantage. To return once more to the story, "A Good Man Is Hard to Find," and the question of why and how that story can be called comic, it may now be clearer that the violence of that story is never completely without a humorous coloring. The early dialogue among the grandmother and June Star and Bailey becomes more than trivial bickering. It now becomes intensely significant that the grandmother has dressed so that anyone coming upon her body after a highway accident could see at once that she was a lady. The violence supercharges, in a manner of speaking, the comedy and this is explicitly illustrated in [T]he Misfit's parting tribute: "'She would of been a good woman . . . if it had been somebody there to shoot her every minute of her life.'"

O'Connor accepted philosophically the fact that some of her readers failed to see her humor. About her audience she wrote: "You discover your audience at the same time and in the same way that you discover your subject; but it is an added blow."[11]

Notes

[1] Flannery O'Connor in a conversation with Robert Drake, August, 1963.

[2] "Some Remarks on Humor," in *The Second Tree from the Corner* (1954), rpt. in *The Comic in Theory and Practice*, eds. John J. Enck, Elizabeth T. Fortner, Alvin Whitley (New York: Appleton-Century-Crofts, 1960), p. 102.

[3] Flannery O'Connor, "On Her Own Work," in *Mystery and Manners*, eds. Sally and Robert Fitzgerald (New York: Farrar, Straus and Giroux, 1957), p. 108.

[4] Louis D. Rubin, ed., *The Comic Imagination in American Literature* (New Brunswick, N.J.: Rutgers Univ. Press, 1973), x.

[5] (Baton Rouge: LSU Press, 1973), pp. 14, 18.

[6] *The Flannery O'Connor Bulletin*, IV (1975), 1–12.

[7] *The Flannery O'Connor Bulletin*, VI (1977), 47–71.

[8] "Some Remarks on Humor," p. 102.

[9] Rubin, "Introduction," pp. 8–13.

[10] Rubin, "The Barber Kept on Shaving," p. 385.

[11] *Mystery and Manners*, p. 118.

A. R. COULTHARD

Flannery O'Connor's
Deadly Conversions

Flannery O'Connor once said, "It seems to me that all good stories are about conversion,"[1] and in fourteen of the nineteen stories collected in *A Good Man Is Hard To Find* (1955) and *Everything That Rises Must Converge* (1965), the protagonist is either redeemed or humbled, making conversion a possibility. O'Connor, however, was well aware of the problem of depicting the mystery of grace in convincing fictional terms.[2] All of her salvation stories contain wonderfully realized scenes, sharply drawn characters, and provocative moral conflicts, but not all of them are successful dramatizations of the believable reality which O'Connor thought every good story must have. O'Connor's letters and the essays and lectures of *Mystery and Manners* testify that writing was just as important to O'Connor as religion, and the unevenness of her redemption stories reflects the inherent difficulty of serving art and theology equally well. Nowhere is this unevenness more evident than in the three stories which link death with redemption.

These stories—"The River," "Greenleaf," and "A Good Man Is Hard To Find" —postulate redemption as occurring almost simultaneously with death, a fact which at first glance may seem to be a literal rendering of the orthodox belief that one has to lose life in order to gain it. However, not one of the protagonists actually chooses to die for spiritual rebirth, so the three untimely deaths must be examined from angles other than the invitingly simple one that the protagonists' sacrifice of life equals affirmation. . . .

"A Good Man Is Hard To Find" is O'Connor's only successful dramatization of the death-salvation theme. The story was one of O'Connor's favorites, and her letters include discussions of it with a variety of correspondents. One of the more amusing is between O'Connor and a professor of English, who, introducing himself as the "spokesman for three members of our department and some ninety university students," sent O'Connor an interpretation of "A Good Man" speculating that beginning with the appeaance of The Misfit, the story is imaginary and that "Bailey, we further believe, identifies himself with The Misfit and so plays two roles in the imaginary last half of the story" (*HB,* 436).

O'Connor responded in an uncharacteristically miffed tone, opening with "The interpretation of your ninety students and three teachers is fantastic and about as far from my intention as it could get to be." O'Connor's letter also includes the widely accepted statement of the spiritual conflict of "A Good Man": "The story is a duel of sorts between the [g]randmother and her superficial beliefs and [T]he Misfit's more profoundly felt involvement with Christ's action which set the world off balance for him" (*HB*, 437).

In spite of the interest in The Misfit O'Connor expressed in this and other letters, the story's moral point is carried by the grandmother, who is another of O'Connor's shallow, complacent women for whom appearance is the only reality. She dresses in her Sunday best for the family's trip to Florida so that "in case of an accident, anyone seeing her dead on the highway would know at once that she was a lady". Her sentimentally naive view of life is devoid of sensitivity. When the family drives past a trouserless Negro boy standing in the doorway of a shack, the old woman gushes, "Oh look at the cute little pickaninny! Wouldn't that make a picture now?" She also displays the mindless vanity typical of O'Connor sinners by adding, "Little niggers in the country don't have things like we do".

Furthermore, the family's predicament traces directly to the old woman's selfishness and stupidity. With the help of the two bratty children, she persuades Bailey to take a dirt-road detour to visit a plantation manor which doesn't even exist, and her cat, which she has smuggled aboard, wraps itself around Bailey's neck and causes him to wreck the car, setting the stage for the appearance of The Misfit and his henchmen in the ominous "big black battered hearse-like automobile." When the old lady blurts, "You're The Misfit!" and The Misfit replies, "It would have been better for all of you, lady, if you hadn't of reckernized me," the reader knows that the hapless family is doomed.

The Misfit's main function lies in the test he brings to the old lady's mindless, benign moral universe. While the death scene during which The Misfit and his boys kill off the entire family one by one is as bone-chilling as any in fiction, O'Connor's interest is, as always, in moral rather than physical horror. She wrote to Andrew Lytle, "There is a moment of grace in most of the stories. . . . Like when the [g]randmother recognizes [T]he Misfit as one of her own children and reaches out to touch him. It's a moment of grace for her anyway—a silly old woman—but it leads him to shoot her. This moment of grace excites the devil to frenzy" (*HB*, 373). In this view of the story, O'Connor sees the old lady as redeemed, in spite of her shallowness, and clearly links The Misfit with Satan.

Not all of O'Connor's comments on the story, however, are this consistent with textual evidence. In a bewildering statement to John Hawkes, O'Connor suggested that the grandmother does not achieve salvation but that The Misfit does:

Grace, to the Catholic way of thinking, can and does use as its medium the imperfect, purely human, and even hypocritical. . . . The Misfit is touched by the Grace that comes through the old lady when she recognizes him as her child, as she has been touched by the Grace that comes through him in his particular suffering. His shooting her is a recoil, a horror at her humanness, but after he has done it and cleaned his glasses, the Grace has worked in him and he pronounces his judgment: she would have been a good woman if *he* had been there every moment of her life. True enough. (*HB*, 389).

O'Connor repeated this view of The Misfit as a sympathetic character in a 1962 letter to Charlotte Gafford: "The Misfit, of course, is a spoiled prophet. As you point out, he could go on to great things" (*HB*, 465).

But The Misfit does not begin to measure up to this positive assessment of his character. One wonders what O'Connor could have had in mind when she posited his shooting the old woman for her "humanness" as a spiritual act; furthermore, quite the opposite of being a guilt-ridden criminal, The Misfit wallows in self-pity. Amazingly, he has named himself The Misfit not because he is a social outcast but "because I can't make what all I done wrong fit what all I gone through in punishment." This from a man who presides over the cold-blooded murder of an entire family, even the baby.

While it is true that The Misfit's meanderings on religion do reflect a "profoundly felt involvement with Christ's action," it is also true that The Misfit has rejected God:

If He did what He said, then it's nothing for you to do but thow away everything and follow Him, and if He didn't, then it's nothing for you to do but enjoy the few minutes you got left the best way you can—by killing somebody or burning down his house or doing some other meanness to him.

Since The Misfit is indeed killing somebody, his decision is clear. He is just as vain as the old lady and much more despicably evil. If the door to salvation remains open a crack for The Misfit, it is because of God's unlimited mercy and The Misfit's statement ending the story. He has told the grandmother that there is "No pleasure but meanness," but when one of his cut-throats says "Some fun!" after the family is disposed of, The Misfit responds, "Shut up, Bobby Lee. It's no real pleasure in life." Robbing and killing just don't seem to be much fun for The Misfit, but this hardly qualifies him for "spoiled prophet" status. Fortunately, the story is much more coherent than O'Connor's comments on it. "A Good Man Is Hard To Find" works theologically not because The Misfit is a potentially good man but because the grandmother develops into a truly good woman.

O'Connor sold the grandmother short when she described her type to John Hawkes: "These old ladies exactly reflect the banalities of the society and the effect is of the comical rather than the seriously evil" (*HB*, 389). The fact that the old woman begs for her life only and not for the family's is hardly comic, nor is the nature of her rejection of religion, once it has been made real to her by the horror of the moment and The Misfit's babbling: "Finally she found herself saying, 'Jesus, Jesus,' meaning, Jesus will help you, but the way she was saying it, it sounded as if she might be cursing." The grandmother hits spiritual bottom when, in a last attempt to save her life, she ingratiatingly denies God to The Misfit by saying, "Maybe He didn't raise the dead."

At this point, the grandmother accepts her death as inevitable, and the narrator describes her as "feeling so dizzy that she sank down in the ditch with her legs twisted under her." Then, with all her vanity burned away by hopelessness, a miracle occurs:

> [His voice seemed about to crack and] . . . the grandmother's head cleared for an instant. She saw the man's face twisted close to her own as if he were going to cry and she murmured, "Why you're one of my babies. You're one of my own children!" She reached out and touched him on the shoulder. The Misfit sprang back as if a snake had bitten him and shot her three times through the chest.

The grandmother's admitting kinship to The Misfit, confirmed by her reaching out and touching him, is dramatic proof that she has seen herself in the "blasting annihilating light" required for redemption.

The old lady is touched not so much by The Misfit's suffering as by his evil. In accepting this miserable, lowly sinner as one of her own children, this once proud lady is admitting to her own sinful nature for the first time, and it is in this epiphany that she finds salvation. The theology of this conclusion is sound, and it is vintage O'Connor: even a silly, self-serving old woman can see the light, with the help of God's mercy and the right kind of pressure.

O'Connor's identification of The Misfit with the devil perfectly fits this reading of the story and explains why he springs back "as if a snake had bitten him" when the old lady touches him. The Misfit has chosen evil and in his inverted Garden of Eden, goodness is the snake. He has no trouble understanding the woman or dealing with her while she is playing by his rules. But once she finds grace, she becomes a threat to all he stands for. She is in a sense visible proof that God did raise the dead, for His power has, before The Misfit's very eyes, transformed a proud sinner into a humble believer. The Misfit's sarcastic remark, "She would [of] been a good woman if it had been somebody there to shoot her every minute of her life," is merely self-defense, his way of continuing to live with what he has become after what he has seen. The Misfit's final remark, "It's no real pleasure in life," merely confirms the futility and stupidity of such a choice. This reading of the climax reveals as perfect a unity as a story can have. That O'Connor at times expressed an opposite view of her conclusion and of The Misfit's role suggests that, at least in this case, her aesthetic instincts were superior to her critical judgment.

In "The Church and the Fiction Writer," O'Connor states, "What the fiction writer will discover, if he discovers anything at all, is that he himself cannot move or mold reality in the interests of abstract truth."[3] But in the conclusions of two of her three stories in which the protagonists pay for grace with their lives, O'Connor does distort reality in the interest of theology. Mrs. May's goring in "Greenleaf" is more contrived than inevitable, and young Harry's drowning in "The River" only slightly less so. In neither story is the death of the protagonist convincingly uplifting or consistently depicted as a spiritual act. Neither do these two stories measure up to O'Connor's requirement that converts first see themselves in a "blasting annihilating light." Extreme callowness rules out the possibility of such a vision for the young protagonist of "The River," and it is absent from "Greenleaf" to the extent that Mrs. May ends up an unconvincing symbol, a mannekin to the faith, rather than a changed human being.

Only in "A Good Man Is Hard To Find" is the death of the protagonist inevitable and her conversion made convincing by dialogue and action. "The River" is an interesting, if flawed, piece of social criticism, and "Greenleaf" is grotesquely amusing, but "A Good Man Is Hard To Find" is the only death-salvation story in which O'Connor equally serves both her God and her muse. The achievement of this masterpiece is enhanced by the relative failure of O'Connor's two other attempts in this difficult genre.

NOTES

[1] Flannery O'Connor, *The Habit of Being*, ed. Sally Fitzgerald (New York: Farrar, 1979), p. 275. Subsequent references to this volume are incorporated into the text of the paper as *HB*.

[2] Flannery O'Connor, *Mystery and Manners*, eds. Sally and Robert Fitzgerald (New York: Farrar, 1969), p. 147.

[3] *Mystery and Manners*, pp. 145–46.

DIXIE LEE HIGHSMITH

Flannery O'Connor's Polite Conversation

Jonathan Swift's *Polite Conversation* is properly titled *A Complete Collection of Genteel and Ingenious Conversation, According to the Most Polite Mode and Method Now Used at Court, and in the Best Companies of England in Three Dialogues.* The satire is evident in the title itself. Wagstaff, the persona, intends to "present a Complete System to the World" containing "a Thousand shining questions, Answers, Repartees, Replies and Rejoinders, fitted to adorn every kind of Discourse that an Assembly of English ladies and Gentlemen, met together for their mutual Entertainment, can possible want. . . . Aside from the absurdity of the project, the real irony lies in the falsity of such language. This compendium of fashionable and meaningless prattle relies on artifice and style rather than genuine meaning for its worth. Appropriateness arises from situation only and language becomes divorced from any reality of thought or feeling. Further, Wagstaff offers his dialogues to remedy the "dangerous Evil" of conversation lag among "select Companies." Thus, in some sense, "polite conversation" becomes meaningless talk for its own sake, or non-language.

When we consider Swift's scrupulous concern with language as a moral indicator, his message is *Polite Conversation* becomes clear. The "polite" use of words is in fact a gross *misuse* of language and reveals only meaninglessness and intellectual vacuity.

In the introduction to the dialogues, we get a fairly good definition of cliché. Wagstaff claims authority for his discourse on the basis of its very emptiness as any sort of *real* language:

> . . . My Collection of polite Discourse . . . hath descended by tradition for
> at least an hundred years, *without any Change in the Phraseology* (emphasis
> added).

That is, like clichés, these phrases have not developed with usage—they are dead and essentially meaningless. Wagstaff is primarily interested in language that is fashionable, transportable, and static. This talk is designed for sound—for keeping a conversational ball rolling—and not to impart, elicit, or reveal knowledge. Real language should serve a revelatory function. It is dynamic and involved with man's ability to articulate and perceive his world.

No pre-formed cataloging of language situations can reflect the depth and complexity of true human discourse. It is important to note as well that Wagstaff offers his volume as an aid to silencing "dull, dry, tedious Story-tellers" and "wrangling Disputers." That effectively removes the influence of literature and rhetoric and again reduces "polite conversation" to mannerly drivel.

One further point should be considered here. Simon Wagstaff, the "Author" of these dialogues, is as pretentious and shallow as the polite conversation he advocates. Throughout the introduction, he continually mentions the price of his volume, the fame he will accrue from it, and the pride he feels both in producing the work and in his own membership in "polite society." He considers himself an authority on language, capable of "improving and polishing all parts of conversation," but at one point admits to and takes pride in being illiterate. He claims that *words* are useless and that his method, presented in the dialogues, will replace the need for books and learning. Polite conversation, and, by extension, language itself becomes artifice, a practiced social habit reflecting at most breeding and training, not meaning.

Even a cursory scanning of Flannery O'Connor's titles reveals her frequent use of cliché and adage. In fact, her characters often speak in strings of pre-formed homilies, old Puritan guidelines transformed into Southern hick dialect. This can be, on the one hand, explained as realism or as the attempt to capture the flavor of the Bible-belt talk O'Connor knew so well. And so it is. This canned language roots her characters in the hard-line Protestant Sunday school morality that pervades the region. But something more than verisimilitude is at work here. When we consider O'Connor's comment in *Mystery and Manners* that the South is not Christ-centered, but Christ-haunted, and her general view that the modern world has largely dismissed spiritual concerns, it becomes obvious that the religious talk of the South has somehow lost its dynamics. The twist is that these clichés turn on themselves, on their speakers, and on readers, causing, generally, a re-evaluation of meaning. The titles are given with a cutting edge, achieved through masterful use of language. Cliché itself, in O'Connor's hands, becomes a metaphor for man's denial of ultimate concerns, for the separation of manners from the mystery which gives them meaning.

Flannery O'Connor often used what might be called "country idiom," both in authorial narration and dialogue, as a method of characterization. Not only does she employ a kind of twentieth-century white Southern "polite conversation," but this language is often religious or moral in nature. More than simply illustrating an abuse of language, the words themselves seem to acquire meaning through the story and offer up a chance for revelation. Thus, even polite conversation can have a dynamic effect on human understanding, can actually be the instrument for religious insight or a vehicle for grace. Language itself can be a key to sacramental vision.

O'Connor was explicit in her belief that an all-informing God is constantly revealed in His creation. Language is of course a part of this creation, but more importantly, it is a part in which man plays an active, creative role. The concept of God's revelation through the Word is an old idea, brought down by O'Connor to the comic and regional to affirm its universality. Humans may speak a "dead" language, but that language can be resurrected by grace.

Moral laxity in O'Connor's characters is represented in various ways, but never so clearly as in the use of religious cliché by essentially non-religious characters. Often this language serves as a mask or façade, or simply as polite social custom; but, in almost every story in which this is the case, at some point the façade crumbles and the character is left to consider his condition in light of his language use. That is, he frequently talks himself into a situation where true meaning is revealed not only in spite of, but through, the use of cliché.

O'Connor claimed that the fiction writer looks for the "peculiar crossroads where time and place and eternity somehow meet." How word and thing are coupled in the human mind is beyond the realm of philosophy, science, or psychology; it is in fact a mystery beyond the power of any determinism to explain.

While O'Connor denied a utilitarian or moral aim to fiction beyond the presentation of reality, that reality was an *ultimate* concern—transcending perception and human knowing and touching mystery. Although Percy's theory of language is, for the most part, a-religious, this kind of ultimate reality lurks behind his interest in man's facility with words. To both writers, language has a kind of supernatural dynamism that can reveal to us what we are essentially while it illumines a larger reality in the face of which we must admit humility and awe. The presentation of a sacramental vision of a continuous and *good* creation, from which we are partially separated, but not entirely removed, is the aim of O'Connor's fiction. The concrete word—the event of speech—has in it the essentials of mystery even as it verifies or negates for us the realities of our perceptions.

O'Connor forces this fact upon the reader with sharp clarity in her use of what Swift called "polite conversation." For even in the human use of "dead" language, or cliché, the action of grace can infuse a new dynamism, blasting the pious use of words and opening again the mysterious function of language to reveal ultimate reality, what O'Connor saw as the Mystery of Truth. Cliché can, often by violence, be made to yield meaning, restoring to language its revelatory function.

In Flannery O'Connor's work, language, even (or perhaps particularly) cliché, has the power of Walker Percy's "piece of news from across the seas." Like O'Connor, Percy considered man as essentially a castaway—someone not really at home in the world even if he does not realize it. That is, man is "displaced." This displacement manifests itself in the restlessness and depression of our age, in the surface interactions of society, in the meaningless talk of modern man. But before the castaway can hear "the piece of news from across the seas" he must recognize and accept his displacement. He must see that he is fundamentally homeless and homesick. He must realize that he awaits just such a piece of news. When O'Connor speaks in *Mystery and Manners* of her hostile audience, she is recognizing the proud and stubborn nature of the castaway. Religious mystery has very little meaning for twentieth-century readers and the prophet's voice is apt to be shrill in order to make the castaway listen to his news. For O'Connor, the most basic human experience was that of human limitation. The suffering of the redemption to which she refers frequently in her letters is the awareness of this limitation, the necessary first step for salvation. This involves a shattering of complacency and pride, a humble recognition of the incompleteness of man's knowledge. Once pride is broken, the actions of mercy and grace— Percy's "news" —can transform the castaway. Grace is in fact the very thing which the castaway has been lacking.

All this might seem far removed from our discussion of polite conversation but actually it is not. The displaced person, because he is free, can refuse or deny the actions of grace indefinitely. He can continually support his own displacement by ignoring it, by concerning himself with physical comfort, by attending to determinisms and psychology. Here, his language will betray him, for he will speak more and more in pious platitudes and clichés. And he will resist any attempt to penetrate that language to discover meaning. He will, in short, continue to delude himself as long as he has fellow castaways willing to assist him. While there is no prophet to intervene, the pious exchange of meaningless language can forestall or eliminate the pull of "news from across the seas." For it is the nature of news that it must have a bearer *and* a hearer. News has direct implications for its receiver, and where these implications are denied outright, no exchange can take place.

Miles Orvell has noted in *Invisible Parade* that several of O'Connor's stories are concerned with characters who are "passive and complacent before the universe—upon whom a 'definition' of self in relation to the mysterious nature of reality is suddenly intruded." We are interested in these intruding agents when they occur in the form of persons who disrupt the situations and lives of the characters in the stories. The conversational exchanges between these characters yield the kind of dynamic force of language we are trying to discover. Also, the "definition of self" that Orvell refers to can often be a re-definition of meaning in language. Thus, the "intrusion" of an outsider can bring about an "intrusion of mystery into the lives of these passive and unsuspecting characters." And mystery restores the dynamics and revelatory function of language to the platitudinous cliché of polite conversation.

The grandmother in "A Good Ma[n] Is Hard To Find" is a "good woman." She professes a proper respect for morality and decorum. She is a lady. And she is a pious user of clichés. As the family excursion begins, the grandmother points out interesting sights along the way in an attempt to instruct her grandchildren. At one point, she notices a black child standing in the doorway of a shack. For the grandmother, the scene is picturesque, a charming reminder of the past. The poverty of the black child's situation is not real to her. Interestingly, this scene is juxtaposed against a comment she had made immediately before. In noting what she called the children's disrespect for their native state, she proclaims that "people did right then." The cliché is an ironic statement on the South's past, on the grandmother's racism, and on her faulty morality. Later, in a comment by the narrator, the grandmother is described as having "a naturally sunny disposition," a statement which we by this time cannot help equating with a kind of mindlessness.

The scene in The Tower includes the first mention of the cliché of the title. When Red Sammy first comes into the restaurant, he begins the meaningless small talk that marks him and the grandmother as sanctimonious. They discuss the corruption of the times and remark that "These days you don't know who to trust." The conversation is so banal and meaningless that the two are practically reduced to simply agreeing with each other. Ironically, Red Sammy says, "It was no use talking about it, she [the grandmother] was exactly right." But of course they do talk, and the polite conversation points to the essence of the story. Red Sammy asserts that "A good man is hard to find." He does not mean this in any real sense—it is just polite talk after all—but the grandmother has already called him a good man and the implication is that they represent two *good* people and, because there are so few *good* people, they see themselves as superior. It is just this kind of unthinking pride that O'Connor wished to expose.

It might be interesting here to contrast Red Sammy and The Misfit. Both men are capable of engaging the grandmother in conversation, but while Red Sammy trades small talk and clichés with her, The Misfit is genuinely presenting his beliefs and forcing the grandmother to defend hers. Both men discuss the question of "goodness" and "what the world is coming to," but for The Misfit these are urgent and real concerns. Red Sammy is rude to his wife, lazy, and complacent. The Misfit is gentlemanly, earnest, and burdened with guilt.

The smug and moralistic grandmother brings down violence upon the family. She has secretly brought the cat along and, after scheming to get Bailey to leave the highway in search of an old mansion she remembered from childhood—which she forgets is located in Tennessee and not Georgia—she upsets the cat's basket and so is responsible for the car accident. Again, it is the grandmother who recognizes The Misfit, a recognition which will cost them their lives. This recognition is twofold: first, she has seen his face in the newspapers; secondly, she later realizes her profound kinship with him.

The grandmother, aside from her mindless and pious talk, is also careless with the truth. She uses language for her own purposes, trying to manipulate her son and The Misfit in order to assume superiority over them. She claims that the car turned over twice, but The Misfit corrects her exaggeration. After she has realized the seriousness of the situation and has been reprimanded by her son, the grandmother begins begging for her life. And the language she uses is the same country talk, the same pious jargon, she has used all along. She cries, "You wouldn't shoot a lady, would you?" and brings out a clean handkerchief to dab her eyes. Her pleading is for her own sake and is based on her worthless idea of gentility. Next she calls The Misfit a "good man" and says that he doesn't look like he has "common blood." The irony here lies in the juxtaposition of these two ideas and in the fact that her concept of "commonness" is mixed up with her idea of her own superiority. "Common blood" also acquires meaning when the "brotherhood of man" is considered in all its implications of shared guilt and responsibility. The grandmother is frantically talking to save her life, but she is still using meaningless and empty words. The Misfit is mannerly and polite, and his words carry a cold weight of meaning. He says, "Nome, I ain't a good man." He is aware of sin and his own sinful nature; the grandmother is not. While The Misfit can talk with the old lady, can even share her idiom, he is not duped by words. He faces himself and his actions squarely and demands that the grandmother do the same.

Still rattling on, the grandmother asks The Misfit to "think how wonderful it would be to settle down and live a comfortable life and not have to think about somebody chasing you all the time." The Misfit's response reveals that he sees the implications of these words more clearly than she does: "Yes'm, somebody is always after you." Meanness and violence are necessary for The Misfit to keep Grace away. Redemption is at all moments possible, but it must be willingly accepted.

After The Misfit runs through the tale of his life, the grandmother still responds piously. She exhorts him to "pray, pray. . . ." But she is speaking out of fear and frenzy, trying to say whatever will save her life. She is not yet talking honestly with The Misfit. She wants to subdue or outwit him and her fervor increases. But genuine meaning and the piety of her words are still far apart. "If you would pray," the old lady says, "Jesus would help you." Again, we don't believe she means this. The Misfit, however, recognizes the power of prayer and has chosen not to seek mercy. He says, "I don't want no hep . . . I'm doing all right by myself."

After the rest of the family is taken off into the woods by Hiram and Bobby Lee, the grandmother experiences a momentary loss of voice. "She wanted to tell him that he must pray. She opened and closed her mouth several times before anything came out." Her pious talk is failing her and when she does speak, to call Jesus' name, "it sounded as if she might be cursing." The Misfit, though not a "good man," is at least aware of the importance of the moral issue of Christ's message. It is not platitude for him, even though he has not accepted the message. The Misfit sees the world in absolutes. The grandmother's views are, to this point, practical and worldly. Her comment, "Maybe he didn't raise the dead," marks another loss of voice—that is, she did not know "what she was saying." Although she cannot see any meaning in her language that transcends her immediate purposes, here she has admitted doubt. I take it that O'Connor means us to consider that doubt a breakdown of pride and complacency—the "lady," the "good woman," is beginning to recognize her own sin, her fallen nature.

The Misfit's cry, "If I had of been there I would of known," presents the dilemma of man: he can only fail when he relies on himself as the measure of Reality. It is also this cry which triggers the grandmother's recognition of kinship with The Misfit—a kinship which begins with original sin and the fall of man and acknowledges that we *are* our brothers' keepers. Her gesture, which incites the crime and indicates the pivotal nature of this scene, is a Christ-like one demonstrating recognition, kinship, love.

MADISON JONES

A Good Man's Predicament
(1984)

Flannery O'Connor's "A Good Man Is Hard to Find" has been for the past decade or more a subject of virtually countless critical readings. Any brilliant work of fiction resists a single interpretation acceptable to everyone, but judging by the variousness and irreconcilability of so many readings of "A Good Man" one might conclude, as R. V. Cassill does, that like the work of Kafka the story "may not be susceptible to exhaustive rational analysis." The suggestion, I believe would be quite apt if applied to a good many O'Connor stories. Not this one, however. If there are in fact authorial lapses, moments when the reader's gaze is led a little awry, they are simply that, lapses, instances of O'Connor nodding.

Much has been made of O'Connor's use of the grotesque, and the vacationing family in "A Good Man" is a case in point. The family members are portrayed almost exclusively in terms of their vices, so much so, it would seem, as to put them at risk of losing entirely not only the reader's sympathy but even his recognition of them as representatively human—a result certain to drain the story of most of its meaning and power. Such is not the result, however. What otherwise must prompt severity in the reader's response is mitigated here by laughter, the transforming element through which human evil is seen in the more tolerable aspect of folly. The author laughs and so do we, and the moral grossness of the family becomes funny to us. This is what engages and sustains our interest in them and, through the effect of distance that humor creates, makes possible our perception of their representative character.

What we see portrayed is increasingly recognizable. Here embodied in this family are standard evils of our culture. Indeed the term "family" is itself a misnomer, for there is no uniting bond. It is each for himself, without respect, without manners. The children, uncorrected, crudely insult their grandmother, and the grandmother for her own selfish ends uses the children against her surly son. The practice of deceit and the mouthing of pietisms are constants in her life, and her praise of the past when good men were easy to find degrades that past by the banality of her memories. Even such memories as she has are not to be depended on; in fact, it is one of her "mis-rememberings" that leads the family to disaster.

But this portrait of unrelieved vulgarity is extended, and by more than implication only, to suggest the world at large. This is the function of the interlude at Red Sammy's barbecue joint where the child June Star does her tap routine and Red Sammy bullies his wife and engages with the grandmother in self-congratulatory conversation about the awfulness of the times and how hard it is to find a "good" man these days. It is hard indeed. In a world unleavened by any presence of the spiritual—a world portrayed, incidentally, in scores of contemporary TV sit-coms—where is a good man to be found? Nowhere, is the answer, though in one way The Misfit himself comes closest to earning the description.

The Misfit is introduced at the very beginning of the story by the grandmother who is using the threat of him, an escaped convict and killer, as a means of getting her own way with her son Bailey. After this The Misfit waits unmentioned in the wings until the portrait of this representative family is complete. His physical entrance into the story, a hardly acceptable coincidence in terms of purely realistic fiction, is in O'Connor's spiritual economy—which determines her technique—like a step in a train of logic. Inert until now, he is nevertheless the conclusion always implicit in the life of the family. Now events produce him in all his terror.

The Misfit comes on the scene of the family's accident in a car that looks like a hearse. The description of his person, generally that of the sinister red-neck of folklore, focuses on a single feature: the silver-rimmed spectacles that give him a scholarly look. This is a clue and a rather pointed one. A scholar is someone who seeks to know the nature of reality and a scholar is what The Misfit was born to be. As The Misfit tells the grandmother:

> "My daddy said I was a different breed of dog from my brothers and sisters. 'You know,' Daddy said, 'it's some that can live their whole life out without asking about it and it's others has to know why it is, and this boy is one of the latters. He's going to be into everything!'"

And in the course of his life he has been into everything:

> "I was a gospel singer for a while," The Misfit said. "I been most everything. Been in the arm service, both land and sea, at home and abroad, been twict married, been an undertaker, been with the railroads, plowed Mother Earth, been in a tornado, seen a man burnt alive oncet" . . . "I even seen a woman flogged," he said.

Life and death, land and sea, war and peace, he has seen it all. And his conclusion, based on his exhaustive experience of the world, is that we are indeed in the "terrible predicament" against which Bailey, who is about to be murdered for no cause, hysterically cries out. "Nobody realizes what this is," Bailey says, but he is wrong. The Misfit knows what it is: a universal condition of meaningless suffering, of punishment that has no intelligible relationship to wrongs done by the victim.

> "I call myself The Misfit," he said, "because I can't make what all I done wrong fit what all I gone through in punishment." . . . "Does it seem right to you, lady, that one is punished a heap and another ain't punished at all?" . . . "No lady." . . . "I found out the crime don't matter. You can do one thing or you can do another, kill a man or take a tire off his car, because sooner or later you're going to forget what it was you done and just be punished for it."

Now The Misfit signs everything and keeps a copy. That way:

> "You'll know what you done and you can hold up the crime to the punishment and see do they match and in the end you'll have something to prove you ain't been treated right."

The Misfit, of course, makes reference here to one significant experience not included in the catalogue previously quoted, but this experience was probably the crucial one. He was sent to the penitentiary for a crime— killing his father—of which he has no memory. In fact he is certain that he did not do it. But they had the papers on him. So, without any consciousness of the crime for which he was being punished, he was "buried alive," as he says. And his description of his confinement, with walls every way he turned, makes an effective image of The Misfit's vision of the world.

The penitentiary experience, however, has a further important thematic significance. It is the very figure of a cardinal doctrine of Christianity, that of Original Sin. Man, conscious or not of the reason, suffers the consequences of Adam's Fall. Guilt is inherited, implicit in a nature severed from God's sustaining grace and submitted to the rule of a Prince who is Darkness. Hence a world deprived of moral order, where irrational suffering prevails: the world that The Misfit so clearly sees with the help of his scholarly glasses. Here, he believes, are the facts, the irremediable facts, of the human condition.

What The Misfit cannot see, or cannot believe in, is any hope of redress for the human condition. He may be haunted, at times tormented, by a vision of Christ raising the dead, but he cannot believe it: he was not there. All that he can believe, really believe, is what his eyes show him: this world without meaning or justice, this prison house where we are confined. Seeing this, what response is fitting? Says The Misfit:

"Then it's nothing for you to do but enjoy the few minutes you got left the best way you can—by killing somebody or burning down his house or doing some other meanness to him. No pleasure but meanness," he said and his voice became almost a snarl.

It is like the response of Satan himself, as Milton envisions it:

Save what is in destroying; other joy
To me is lost.

But release for hate of an unjust creation is at best an illusory pleasure. "It's no real pleasure in life," The Misfit says, after the carnage is complete.

What has driven The Misfit to his homicidal condition is his powerful but frustrated instinct for meaning and justice. It may be inferred that this same instinct is what has produced his tormenting thoughts about Christ raising the dead, making justice where there is none. If only he could have been there when it happened, then he could have believed.

"I wisht I had of been there," he said, hitting the ground with his fist. "It ain't right I wasn't there because if I had of been there I would of known. Listen, lady," he said in a high voice, "if I had of been there I would of known and I wouldn't be like I am now."

It is torment to think of what might have been, that under other circumstances he would have been able to believe and so escape from the self he has become. In light of this it is possible to read The Misfit's obscure statement that Jesus "thown everything off balance," as meaning this: that it would have been better, for the world's peace and his own, if no haunting doubt about the awful inevitability of man's condition ever had been introduced. In any case it could only be that doubt has made its contribution to the blighting of The Misfit's soul.

But doubts like this are not enough to alter The Misfit's vision. In the modern manner he believes what he can see with his eyes only, and his eyes have a terrible rigor. It is this rigor that puts him at such a distance from the grandmother who is one of the multitude "that can live their whole life without asking about it," that spend their lives immersed in a world of platitudes which they have never once stopped to scrutinize. This, his distinction from the vulgarians whom the grandmother represents, his honesty, is the source of The Misfit's pride. It is why, when the grandmother calls him a "good" man, he answers: "Nome, I ain't a good man," . . . "but I ain't the worst in the world neither." And it is sufficient reason for the violent response that causes him so suddenly and unexpectedly to shoot the grand-mother. Here is what happens, beginning with the grandmother's mur-mured words to The Misfit:

> "Why, you're one of my babies. You're one of my own children!" She reached out and touched him on the shoulder. The Misfit sprang back as if a snake had bitten him and shot her three times through the chest.

Given The Misfit's image of himself, her words and her touching, blessing him, amount to intolerable insult, for hereby she includes him among the world's family of vulgarians. One of her children, her kind, indeed!

This reason for The Misfit's action is, I believe, quite sufficient to ex-plain it, even though Flannery O'Connor, discussing the story in *Mystery and Manners,* implies a different explanation. The grandmother's words to The Misfit and her touching him, O'Connor says, are a gesture represent-ing the intrusion of a moment of grace. So moved, the grandmother recog-nizes her responsibility for this man and the deep kinship between them. O'Connor goes on to say that perhaps in time to come The Misfit's memory of the grandmother's gesture will become painful enough to turn him into the prophet he was meant to be. Seen this way, through the author's eyes, we must infer an explanation other than my own for The Misfit's action. This explanation would envision The Misfit's sudden violence as caused by his dismayed recognition of the presence in the grandmother of a phenom-enon impossible to reconcile with his own view of what is real. Thus The Misfit's act can be seen as a striking out in defense of a version of reality to whose logic he has so appallingly committed himself.

Faced with mutually exclusive interpretations of a fictional event, a reader must accept the evidence of the text in preference to the testimonial of the author. And where the text offers a realistic explanation as opposed to one based on the supernatural, a reader must find the former the more persuasive. *If* the two are in fact mutually exclusive. And *if,* of course, it is true that the acceptability of the author's explanation does in fact depend upon the reader's belief in the supernatural. As to this second condition, it is a measure of O'Connor's great gift that the story offers a collateral ba-sis for understanding grace that is naturalistic in character. This grace may be spelled in lower case letters but the fictional consequence is the same. For sudden insight is quite within the purview of rationalistic psychology, provided only that there are intelligible grounds for it. And such grounds are present in the story. They are implicit in the logic that connects the grandmother and The Misfit, that makes of The Misfit "one of my own children." In the hysteria caused by the imminence of her death, which strips her of those banalities by which she has lived, the grandmother quite believably discovers this connection. And so with the terms of The Misfit's sudden violence. His own tormenting doubt, figured in those preceding moments when he cries out and hits the ground, has prepared him. Supernatural grace or not, The Misfit in this moment sees it as such, and strikes.

These two, the author's and my own, are quite different explanations of The Misfit's sudden violence. Either, I believe, is reasonable, though surely the nod should go to the one that more enriches the story's theme. *If* the two are mutually exclusive. I believe, however, that they are not. Such a mixture of motives, in which self-doubt and offended pride both participate, should put no strain on the reader's imagination. And seen together each one may give additional dimension to the story.

"A Good Man Is Hard to Find" is perhaps Flannery O'Connor's finest story—coherent, powerfully dramatic, relentless, and unique. In essence it is a devastating sermon against the faithlessness of modern generations, man bereft of the spirit. This condition, portrayed in the grossness of the vacationing family, barely relieved by the pious and sentimental prattle of the grandmother, produces its own terror. The Misfit enters, not by coincidence but by the logic implicit in lives made grotesque when vision has departed. He, O'Connor tells us, is the fierce avenger our souls beget upon our innocent nihilism.

FLANNERY O'CONNOR

The Habit of Being

[Editor Sally Fitzgerald provides this background information.]
A Professor of English had sent Flannery the following letter: "I am writing as spokesman for three members of our department and some ninety university students in three classes who for a week now have been discussing your story 'A Good Man Is Hard to Find.' We have debated at length several possible interpretations, none of which fully satisfies us. In general we believe that the appearance of The Misfit is not 'real' in the same sense that the incidents of the first half of the story are real. Bailey, we believe, imagines the appearance of The Misfit, whose

activities have been called to his attention on the night before the trip and again during the stopover at the roadside restaurant. Bailey, we further believe, identifies himself with The Misfit and so plays two roles in the imaginary last half of the story. But we cannot, after great effort, determine the point at which reality fades into illusion or reverie. Does the accident literally occur, or is it a part of Bailey's dream? Please believe me when I say we are not seeking an easy way out of our difficulty. We admire your story and have examined it with great care, but we are convinced that we are missing something important which you intended for us to grasp. We will all be very grateful if you comment on the interpretation which I have outlined above and if you will give us further comments about your intention in writing 'A Good Man Is Hard to Find.'"

She replied:

To a Professor of English

28 March 61

The interpretation of your ninety students and three teachers is fantastic and about as far from my intentions as it could get to be. If it were a legitimate interpretation, the story would be little more than a trick and its interest would be simply for abnormal psychology. I am not interested in abnormal psychology.

There is a change of tension from the first part of the story to the second where The Misfit enters, but this is no lessening of reality. This story is, of course, not meant to be realistic in the sense that it portrays the everyday doings of people in Georgia. It is stylized and its conventions are comic even though its meaning is serious.

Bailey's only importance is as the grandmother's boy and the driver of the car. It is the grandmother who first recognizes The Misfit and who is most concerned with him throughout. The story is a duel of sorts between the grandmother and her superficial beliefs and The Misfit's more profoundly felt involvement with Christ's action which set the world off balance for him.

The meaning of a story should go on expanding for the reader the more he thinks about it, but meaning cannot be captured in an interpretation. If teachers are in the habit of approaching a story as if it were a research problem for which any answer is believable so long as it is not obvious, then I think students will never learn to enjoy fiction. Too much interpretation is certainly worse than too little, and where feeling for a story is absent, theory will not supply it.

My tone is not meant to be obnoxious. I am in a state of shock.

FLANNERY O'CONNOR

On Her Own Work
(1969)

A Reasonable Use of the Unreasonable

Last fall* I received a letter from a student who said she would be "graciously appreciative" if I would tell her "just what enlightenment" I expected her to get from each of my stories. I suspect she had a paper to write. I wrote her back to forget about the enlightenment and just try to enjoy them. I knew that was the most unsatisfactory answer I could have given because, of course, she didn't want to enjoy them, she just wanted to figure them out.

In most English classes the short story has become a kind of literary specimen to be dissected. Every time a story of mine appears in a freshman anthology, I have a vision of it, with its little organs laid open, like a frog in a bottle.

I realize that a certain amount of this what-is-the-significance has to go on, but I think something has gone wrong in the process when, for so many students, the story becomes simply a problem to be solved, something which you evaporate to get Instant Enlightenment.

A story really isn't any good unless it successfully resists paraphrase, unless it hangs on and expands in the mind. Properly, you analyze to enjoy, but it's equally true that to analyze with any discrimination, you have to have enjoyed already, and I think that the best reason to hear a story read is that it should stimulate that primary enjoyment.

I don't have any pretensions to being an Aeschylus or Sophocles and providing you in this story with a cathartic experience out of your mythic background, though this story I'm going to read certainly calls up a good deal of the South's mythic background, and it should elicit from you a degree of pity and terror, even though its way of being serious is a comic one. I do think, though, that like the Greeks, you should know what is going to happen in this story so that any element of suspense in it will be transferred from its surface to its interior.

From *Mystery and Manners*, ed. Sally and Robert Fitzgerald (New York: Farrar, Straus and Giroux, 1969), 107–114.

* I.e., in 1962. These remarks were made by Flannery O'Connor at Hollins College, Virginia, to introduce a reading of her story, "A Good Man Is Hard to Find," on October 14, 1963.

I would be most happy if you had already read it, happier still if you knew it well, but since experience has taught me to keep my expectations along these lines modest, I'll tell you that this is the story of a family of six which, on its way driving to Florida, gets wiped out by an escaped convict who calls himself The Misfit. The family is made up of the grandmother and her son, Bailey, and his children, John Wesley and June Star and the baby, and there is also the cat and the children's mother. The cat is named Pitty Sing, and the grandmother is taking him with them, hidden in a basket.

Now I think it behooves me to try to establish with you the basis on which reason operates in this story. Much of my fiction takes its character from a reasonable use of the unreasonable, though the reasonableness of my use of it may not always be apparent. The assumptions that underlie this use of it, however, are those of the central Christian mysteries. These are assumptions to which a large part of the modern audience takes exception. About this I can only say that there are perhaps other ways than my own in which this story could be read, but none other by which it could have been written. Belief, in my own case anyway, is the engine that makes perception operate.

The heroine of this story, the grandmother, is in the most significant position life offers the Christian. She is facing death. And to all appearances she, like the rest of us, is not too well prepared for it. She would like to see the event postponed. Indefinitely.

I've talked to a number of teachers who use this story in class and who tell their students that the grandmother is evil, that in fact, she's a witch, even down to the cat. One of these teachers told me that his students, and particularly his Southern students, resisted this interpretation with a certain bemused vigor, and he didn't understand why. I had to tell him that they resisted it because they all had grandmothers or great-aunts just like her at home, and they knew, from personal experience, that the old lady lacked comprehension, but that she had a good heart. The Southerner is usually tolerant of those weaknesses that proceed from innocence, and he knows that a taste for self-preservation can be readily combined with the missionary spirit.

The same teacher was telling his students that morally The Misfit was several cuts above the grandmother. He had a really sentimental attachment to The Misfit. But then a prophet gone wrong is almost always more interesting than your grandmother, and you have to let people take their pleasures where they find them.

It is true that the old lady is a hypocritical old soul; her wits are no match for The Misfit's, nor is her capacity for grace equal to his; yet I think the unprejudiced reader will feel that the grandmother has a special kind of triumph in this story which instinctively we do not allow to someone altogether bad.

I often ask myself what makes a story work, and what makes it hold up as a story, and I have decided that it is probably some action, some gesture of a character that is unlike any other in the story, one which indicates where the real heart of the story lies. This would have to be an action or a gesture which was both totally right and totally unexpected; it would have to be one that was both in character and beyond character; it would have to suggest both the world and eternity. The action or gesture I'm talking about would have to be on the anagogical level, that is, the level which has to do with the Divine life and our participation in it. It would be a gesture that transcended any neat allegory that might have been intended or any pat moral categories a reader could make. It would be a gesture which somehow made contact with mystery.

There is a point in this story where such a gesture occurs. The grandmother is at last alone, facing The Misfit. Her head clears for an instant and she realizes, even in her limited way, that she is responsible for the man before her and joined to him by ties of kinship which have their roots deep in the mystery she has been merely prattling about so far. And at this point, she does the right thing, she makes the right gesture.

I find that students are often puzzled by what she says and does here, but I think myself that if I took out this gesture and what she says with it, I would have no story. What was left would not be worth your attention. Our age not only does not have a very sharp eye for the almost imperceptible intrusions of grace, it no longer has much feeling for the nature of the violences which precede and follow them. The devil's greatest wile, Baudelaire has said, is to convince us that he does not exist.

I suppose the reasons for the use of so much violence in modern fiction will differ with each writer who uses it, but in my own stories I have found that violence is strangely capable of returning my characters to reality and preparing them to accept their moment of grace. Their heads are so hard that almost nothing else will do the work. This idea, that reality is something to which we must be returned at considerable cost, is one which is seldom understood by the casual reader, but it is one which is implicit in the Christian view of the world.

I don't want to equate The Misfit with the devil. I prefer to think that, however unlikely this may seem, the old lady's gesture, like the mustard-seed, will grow to be a great crow-filled tree in The Misfit's heart, and will be enough of a pain to him there to turn him into the prophet he was meant to become.[1] But that's another story.

This story has been called grotesque, but I prefer to call it literal. A good story is literal in the same sense that a child's drawing is literal. When a child draws, he doesn't intend to distort but to set down exactly what he sees, and as his gaze is direct, he sees the lines that create motion. Now the lines of motion that interest the writer are usually invisible. They are lines of spiritual motion. And in this story you should be on the lookout for such things as the action of grace in the grandmother's soul, and not for the dead bodies.

We hear many complaints about the prevalence of violence in modern fiction, and it is always assumed that this violence is a bad thing and meant to be an end in itself. With the serious writer, violence is never an end in itself. It is the extreme situation that best reveals what we are essentially, and I believe these are times when writers are more interested in what we are essentially than in the tenor of our daily lives. Violence is a force which can be used for good or evil, and among other things taken by it is the kingdom of heaven. But regardless of what can be taken by it, the man in the violent situation reveals those qualities least dispensable in his personality, those qualities which are all he will have to take into eternity with him; and since the characters in this story are all on the verge of eternity, it is appropriate to think of what they take with them. In any case, I hope that if you consider these points in connection with the story, you will come to see it as something more than an account of a family murdered on the way to Florida.

NOTE

[1]   See Matthew 13:31–32; Mark 4:31–32; Luke 13:19 [Ed.'s note].

J. O. TATE

A Good Source Is Not So Hard To Find

The mounting evidence of O'Connor's use of items from the Milledgeville and Atlanta newspapers will interest those who realize that these sources, in and of themselves, have nothing to do with the Gothic, the grotesque, the American Romance tradition, Southwestern humor, Southern literature, adolescent aggression, the New Hermeneutics, the anxiety of influence, structuralism, pentecostal Gnosticism, medieval theology, Christian humanism, existentialism, or the Roman Catholic Church.

I. On "The Misfit" as Name and Word

The text of an Atlanta *Constitution* article of November 6, 1952, p. 29, identifies for us the source of a celebrated sobriquet. This newspaper reference was reprinted in *The Flannery O'Connor Bulletin*, Vol. III, Autumn 1974. The headline says enough: "'The Misfit' Robs Office,/Escapes With $150." Flannery O'Connor took a forgotten criminal's alias and used it for larger purposes: *her* Misfit was out of place in a grander way than the original. But we should not forget O'Connor's credentials as "a literalist of the imagination." There is always "a little lower layer." She meant to mock pop psychology by exploiting the original Misfit's exploitation of a socio-psychological "excuse" for aberrant behavior. But even a little lower: the original meaning of the word "misfit" has to do with clothing. We should not fail, therefore, to note that The Misfit's "borrowed" blue jeans are too tight. He leaves the story, of course, wearing Bailey's shirt.

II. On the Identity and Destiny of the Original Misfit

By November 13, 1952, The Misfit had been apprehended; he had also advanced himself to page three of the Atlanta *Journal.* The Misfit was a twenty-five-year old named James C. Yancey. He "was found to be of un-sound mind" and committed to the state mental hospital at—Milledgeville. Where else?

III. On The Misfit's Notoriety, Peregrinations, Good Manners, Eye-glasses, Companions, and Mental Hygiene

The original Misfit was, as criminals go, small potatoes. He was an un-ambitious thief, no more. O'Connor took nothing from him but his impos-ing signature. But it just so happens that there was another well-publicized criminal aloose in Tennessee and Georgia just before the time that O'Con-nor appropriated The Misfit's name. This other hold-up artist had four im-portant qualities in common with *her* Misfit. First, he inspired a certain amount of terror through several states. Second, he had, or claimed to have, a certain *politesse.* Third, he wore spectacles. Fourth, he had two accom-plices, in more than one account.

James Francis ("Three-Gun") Hill, the sinister celebrity of the front pages, much more closely resembles the object of the grandmother's warn-ings than the original Misfit. Various articles tell of "a fantastic record of 26 kidnappings in four states, as many robberies, 10 car thefts, and a climac-tic freeing of four Florida convicts from a prison gang—all in two kaleido-scopic weeks." He had advanced "from an obscure hoodlum to top billing as a public enemy" (The Atlanta *Constitution*, Nov. 1, p. 1). Such headlines as the grandmother had in mind screamed of Hill (though not in the sports section that Bailey was reading): Maniac's Gang Terrorizes Hills (*Constitution*, Oct. 24, p. 2, from Sparta, Tenn.); Search for Kidnap-Robbery Trio/ Centers in Atlanta and Vicinity (Oct. 25, p. 1, from Atlanta); Chattanooga/ Is Focal Point/ For Manhunt (Oct. 27, p. 26); 2nd of Terror/ Gang Seized/ In Florida/ Pal Said Still/ In Atlanta Area (Oct. 29, p. 32); Self-Styled 3-Gun Maniac Frees/ 4 Road Gang Convicts at Gunpoint (Oct. 31, p. 1, from Bartow, Florida). It is quite clear that O'Connor, imagining through the grandmother's point of view, was, like the newspapers, assuming an Atlanta locale and orientation. The southward trip was in the same direction as Hill's last run.

The article of Oct. 24 gives us a bit of color: "A fantastic band of highwaymen, led by a self-styled 'maniac' who laughed weirdly while he looted his victims, spread terror through the Cumberland hills today. . . . [The leader] boasted that he had escaped from the Utah State Prison and 'killed two people'. . . . 'They call me a three-gun maniac, and brother, they got the picture straight,' the head bandit was quoted by victims." The Oct. 31 article hints at the rustic setting of O'Connor's story: ". . . [T]he escapers and Hill . . . drove up a dead-end road and abandoned the car. They fled into thick woods on foot. . . ."

The *Constitution* of Nov. 1 speaks of Hill on the front page as "the bespectacled, shrunken-cheeked highwayman." A later article gives us, as it gave O'Connor, a clue to her Misfit's respectful modes of address: "Good afternoon . . . I pre-chate that, lady . . . Nome . . . I'm sorry I don't have on a shirt before you ladies . . . Yes'm . . ." etc. We read of the trial of "Accused kidnapper, James Francis (Three-Gun) Hill, who says he's a 'gentleman-bandit' because 'I didn't cuss in front of ladies. . . .'" This Associated Press wire story from Chattanooga was on p. 26 of the Nov. 13 Atlanta *Journal*.

The *Constitution* of the same date says "Hearing Delayed for 'Maniac' Hill and 2 Cronies," and goes on to mention "James Francis Hill, self-styled 'three-gun maniac.'" We may observe that both Yancey and Hill were referred to in the newspapers as "self-styled," an arresting phrase perhaps to an author attuned to extravagances of self. I think we may also recognize here the genesis of Hiram and Bobby Lee.

The result of Hill's plea of guilty was perhaps not as forthright as his intention: "'Maniac' Hill/ Is Adjudged/ Incompetent" (*Constitution*, Nov. 18). Like Yancey, The Misfit, Hill was sent to a mental institution—in Tennessee, this time. (His cronies were sentenced to jail.) The diagnosis of both Yancey and Hill as mentally ill may have suggested O'Connor's Misfit's experiences with the "head-doctor."

IV. On The Misfit, Memory, and Guilt

The fictional Misfit was not easily freudened: he knew perfectly well that he had not killed his daddy. Yet he insisted there was no balance between guilt and punishment—if memory served.

The issues of accuracy of memory, consciousness of guilt, and conscience were also raised in an odd "human-interest" story that was published in those same days when O'Connor was gathering so much material from the newspapers. The Misfit's claim that he was punished for crimes he did not remember may have been inspired by this account of a man who was *not* punished for a crime he *did* remember—but remembered wrongly.

The *Journal* of Nov. 5, 1952 carried the article, written from Brookhaven, New York, on page 12: "'Murder' Didn't Happen,/ House Painter Free." Louis Roberts had shot a policeman in 1928; he assumed he had killed him. Over twenty years later, his conscience finally forced him to confess. When his tale was investigated, it was discovered that the policeman had survived after all. There was no prosecution for, as an authority was quoted as saying, "His conscience has punished him enough."

ALICE WALKER

Beyond the Peacock:
The Reconstruction of
Flannery O'Connor
(1975)

It was after a poetry reading I gave at a recently desegregated college in Georgia that someone mentioned that in 1952 Flannery O'Connor and I had lived within minutes of each other on the same Eatonton-to-Milledgeville road. I was eight years old in 1952 (she would have been 28) and we moved away from Milledgeville after less than a year. Still, since I have loved her work for many years, the coincidence of our having lived near each other intrigued me, and started me thinking of her again.

As a college student in the sixties I read her books endlessly, scarcely conscious of the difference between her racial and economic background and my own, but put them away in anger when I discovered that, while I was reading O'Connor—Southern, Catholic, and white—there were other women writers—some Southern, some religious, all black—I had not been allowed to know. For several years, while I searched for, found, and studied black women writers, I deliberately shut O'Connor out, feeling almost ashamed that she had reached me first. And yet, even when I no longer read her, I missed her, and realized that though the rest of America might not mind, having endured it so long, I would never be satisfied with a segregated literature. I would have to read Zora [Neale] Hurston *and* Flannery O'Connor, Nella Larsen *and* Carson McCullers, Jean Toomer *and* William Faulkner, before I could begin to feel *well* read at all.

I thought it might be worthwhile, in 1974, to visit the two houses, Flannery O'Connor's and mine, to see what could be learned twenty-two years after we moved away and ten years after her death. It seemed right to go to my old house first—to set the priorities of vision, so to speak—and then to her house, to see, at the very least, whether her peacocks would still be around. To this bit of nostalgic exploration I invited my mother, who, curious about peacocks and abandoned houses, if not about literature and writers, accepted.

In her shiny new car, which at sixty-one she has learned to drive, we cruised down the wooded Georgia highway to revisit our past.

At the turnoff leading to our former house, we face a fence, a gate, a NO TRESPASSING sign. The car will not fit through the gate and beyond the gate is muddy pasture. It shocks me to remember that when we lived here we lived, literally, in a pasture. It is a memory I had repressed. Now, for a moment, it frightens me.

"Do you think we should enter?" I ask.

But my mother has already opened the gate. To her, life has no fences, except, perhaps, religious ones, and these we have decided not to discuss. We walk through pines rich with vines, fluttering birds, and an occasional wild azalea showing flashes of orange. The day is bright with spring, the sky cloudless, the road rough and clean.

"I would like to see old man Jenkins [who was our landlord] come bothering me about some trespassing," she says, her head extremely up. "He never did pay us for the crop we made for him in fifty-two."

After five minutes of leisurely walking, we are again confronted with a fence, fastened gate, POSTED signs. Again my mother ignores all three, unfastens the gate, walks through.

"He never gave me my half of the calves I raised that year either," she says. And I chuckle at her memory and her style.

Now we are facing a large green rise. To our left calves are grazing; beyond them there are woods. To our right there is the barn we used, looking exactly as it did twenty-two years ago. It is high and weathered silver and from it comes the sweet scent of peanut hay. In front of it, a grove of pecans. Directly in front of us over the rise is what is left of the house.

"Well," says my mother, "it's still standing. And," she adds with wonder, "just look at my daffodils!"

In twenty-two years they have multiplied and are now blooming from one side of the yard to the other. It is a typical abandoned sharefarmer shack. Of the four-room house only two rooms are left; the others have rotted away. These two are filled with hay.

Considering the sad state of the house it is amazing how beautiful its setting is. There is not another house in sight. There are hills, green pastures, a ring of bright trees, and a family of rabbits hopping out of our way. My mother and I stand in the yard remembering. I remember only misery: going to a shabby segregated school that was once the state prison and that had, on the second floor, the large circular print of the electric chair that had stood there; almost stepping on a water moccasin on my way home from carrying water to my family in the fields; losing Phoebe, my cat, because we left this place hurriedly and she could not be found in time.

"Well, old house," my mother says, smiling in such a way that I almost see her rising, physically, above it, "one good thing you gave us. It was right here that I got my first washing machine!"

In fact, the only pleasant thing I recall from that year was a field we used to pass on our way into the town of Milledgeville. It was like a painting by someone who loved tranquillity. In the foreground near the road the green field was used as pasture for black-and-white cows that never seemed to move. Then, farther away, there was a steep hill partly covered with kudzu—dark and lush and creeping up to cover and change fantastically the shapes of the trees. . . . When we drive past it now, it looks the same. Even the cows could be the same cows—though now I see that they *do* move, though not very fast and never very far.

What I liked about this field as a child was that in my life of nightmares about electrocutions, lost cats, and the surprise appearance of snakes, it represented beauty and unchanging peace.

"Of course," I say to myself, as we turn off the main road two miles from my old house, "that's Flannery's field." The instructions I've been given place her house on the hill just beyond it.

There is a garish new Holiday Inn directly across Highway 441 from Flannery O'Connor's house, and, before going up to the house, my mother and I decide to have something to eat there. Twelve years ago I could not have bought lunch for us at such a place in Georgia, and I feel a weary delight as I help my mother off with her sweater and hold out a chair by the window for her. The white people eating lunch all around us—staring though trying hard not to—form a blurred backdrop against which my mother's face is especially sharp. *This* is the proper perspective, I think, biting into a corn muffin; no doubt about it.

As we sip iced tea we discuss O'Connor, integration, the inferiority of the corn muffins we are nibbling, and the care and raising of peacocks.

"Those things will sure eat up your flowers," my mother says, explaining why she never raised any.

"Yes," I say, "but they're a lot prettier than they'd be if somebody human had made them, which is why this lady liked them." This idea has only just occurred to me, but having said it, I believe it is true. I sit wondering why I called Flannery O'Connor a lady. It is a word I rarely use and usually by mistake, since the whole notion of ladyhood is repugnant to me. I can imagine O'Connor at a Southern social affair, looking very polite and being very bored, making mental notes of the absurdities of the evening. Being white she would automatically have been eligible for ladyhood, but I cannot believe she would ever really have joined.

"She must have been a Christian person then," says my mother. "She believed He made everything." She pauses, looks at me with tolerance but also as if daring me to object: "And she was *right*, too."

"She was a Catholic," I say, "which must not have been comfortable in the Primitive Baptist South, and more than any other writer she believed in everything, including things she couldn't see."

"Is that why you like her?" she asks.

"I like her because she could *write*," I say.

"'Flannery' sounds like something to eat," someone said to me once. The word always reminds me of flannel, the material used to make nightgowns and winter shirts. It is very Irish, as were her ancestors. Her first name was Mary, but she seems never to have used it. Certainly "Mary O'Connor" is short on mystery. She was an Aries, born March 25, 1925. When she was sixteen, her father died of lupus, the disease that, years later, caused her own death. After her father died, O'Connor and her mother, Regina O'Connor, moved from Savannah, Georgia, to Milledgeville, where they lived in a townhouse built for Flannery O'Connor's grandfather, Peter Cline. This house, called "the Cline house," was built by slaves who made the bricks by hand. O'Connor's biographers are always impressed by this fact, as if it adds the blessed sign of aristocracy, but whenever I read it I think that those slaves were some of my own relatives, toiling in the stifling middle-Georgia heat, to erect her grandfather's house, sweating and suffering the swarming mosquitoes as the house rose slowly, brick by brick.

Whenever I visit antebellum homes in the South, with their spacious rooms, their grand staircases, their shaded back windows that, without the thickly planted trees, would look out onto the now vanished slave quarters in the back, this is invariably my thought. I stand in the backyard gazing up at the windows, then stand at the windows inside looking down into the backyard, and between the me that is on the ground and the me that is at the windows, History is caught.

O'Connor attended local Catholic schools and then Georgia Women's College. In 1945 she received a fellowship to the Writer's Workshop at the University of Iowa. She received her M.A. in 1947. While still a student she wrote stories that caused her to be recognized as a writer of formidable talent and integrity of craft. After a stay at Yaddo, the artists' colony in up-state New York, she moved to a furnished room in New York City. Later she lived and wrote over a garage at the Connecticut home of Sally and Robert Fitzgerald, who became, after her death, her literary executors.

Although, as Robert Fitzgerald states in the preface to O'Connor's *Everything That Rises Must Converge,* "Flannery was out to be a writer on her own and had no plans to go back to live in Georgia," staying out of Georgia for good was not possible. In December of 1950 she experienced a peculiar heaviness in her "typing arms." On the train home for the Christmas holidays she became so ill she was hospitalized immediately. It was disseminated lupus. In the fall of 1951, after nine wretched months in the hospital, she returned to Milledgeville. Because she could not climb the stairs at the Cline house her mother brought her to their country house, Andalusia, about five miles from town. Flannery O'Connor lived there with her mother for the next thirteen years. The rest of her life.

The word *lupus* is Latin for "wolf," and is described as "that which eats into the substance." It is a painful, wasting disease, and O'Connor suffered not only from the disease—which caused her muscles to weaken and her body to swell, among other things—but from the medicine she was given to fight the disease, which caused her hair to fall out and her hipbones to meet. Still, she managed—with the aid of crutches from 1955 on—to get about and to write, and left behind more than three dozen [sic] superb short stories, most of them prizewinners, two novels, and a dozen or so brilliant essays and speeches. Her book of essays, *Mystery and Manners,* which is primarily concerned with the moral imperatives of the serious writer of fiction, is the best of its kind I have ever read.

"When you make these trips back south," says my mother, as I give the smiling waitress my credit card, "just what is it exactly that you're looking for?"

"A wholeness," I reply.

"You look whole enough to me," she says.

"No," I answer, "because everything around me is split up, deliberately split up. History split up, literature split up, and people are split up too. It makes people do ignorant things. For example, one day I was invited to speak at a gathering of Mississippi librarians and before I could get started, one of the authorities on Mississippi history and literature got up and said she really *did* think Southerners wrote so well because 'we' lost the war. She was white, of course, but half the librarians in the room were black."

"I bet she was real old," says my mother. "They're the only ones still worrying over that war."

"So I got up and said no, 'we' didn't lose the war. '*You* all' lost the war. And you all's loss was our gain."

"Those old ones will just have to die out," says my mother.

"Well," I say, "I believe that the truth about any subject only comes when all the sides of the story are put together, and all their different meanings make one new one. Each writer writes the missing parts to the other writer's story. And the whole story is what I'm after."

"Well, I doubt if you can ever get the *true* missing parts of anything away from the white folks," my mother says softly, so as not to offend the waitress who is mopping up a nearby table; "they've sat on the truth so long by now they've mashed the life out of it."

"O'Connor wrote a story once called 'Everything That Rises Must Converge.'"

"What?"

"Everything that goes up comes together, meets, becomes one thing. Briefly, the story is this: an old white woman in her fifties—"

"That's not old! I'm older than that, and I'm not old!"

"Sorry. This middle-aged woman gets on a bus with her son, who likes to think he is a Southern liberal . . . he looks for a black person to sit next to. This horrifies his mother, who, though not old, has old ways. She is wearing a very hideous, very expensive hat, which is purple and green."

"Purple and *green?*"

"Very expensive. *Smart.* Bought at the best store in town. She says, 'With a hat like this, I won't meet myself coming and going.' But in fact, soon a large black woman, whom O'Connor describes as looking something like a gorilla, gets on the bus with a little boy, and she is wearing this same green-and-purple hat. Well, our not-so-young white lady is horrified, out*done.*"

"I *bet* she was. Black folks have money to buy foolish things with too, now."

"O'Connor's point exactly! Everything that rises, must converge."

"Well, the green-and-purple hats people will have to converge without me."

"O'Connor thought that the South, as it became more 'progressive,' would become just like the North. Culturally bland, physically ravished, and, where the people are concerned, well, you wouldn't be able to tell one racial group from another. Everybody would want the same things, like the same things, and everybody would be reduced to wearing, symbolically, the same green-and-purple hats."

"And do you think this is happening?"

"I do. But that is not the whole point of the story. The white woman, in an attempt to save her pride, chooses to treat the incident of the identical hats as a case of monkey-see, monkey-do. She assumes she is not the monkey, of course. She ignores the idiotic-looking black woman and begins instead to flirt with the woman's son, who is small and black and *cute.* She fails to notice that the black woman is glowering at her. When they all get off the bus she offers the little boy a 'bright new penny.' And the child's mother knocks the hell out of her with her pocketbook."

"I bet she carried a large one."

"Large, and full of hard objects."

"Then what happened? Didn't you say the white woman's son was with her?"

"He had tried to warn his mother. 'These new Negroes are not like the old,' he told her. But she never listened. He thought he hated his mother until he saw her on the ground, then he felt sorry for her. But when he tried to help her, she didn't know him. She'd retreated in her mind to a historical time more congenial to her desires. 'Tell Grandpapa to come get me,' she says. Then she totters off, alone, into the night."

"Poor *thing,*" my mother says sympathetically of this horrid woman, in a total identification that is *so* Southern and *so* black.

"That's what her son felt, too, and *that* is how you know it is a Flannery O'Connor story. The son has been changed by his mother's experience. He understands that, though she is a silly woman who has tried to live in the past, she is also a pathetic creature and so is he. But it is too late to tell her about this because she is stone crazy."

"What did the black woman do after she knocked the white woman down and walked away?"

"O'Connor chose not to say, and that is why, although this is a good story, it is, to me, only half a story. *You* might know the other half. . . ."

"Well, I'm not a writer, but there *was* an old white woman I once wanted to strike . . ." she begins.

"Exactly," I say.

I discovered O'Connor when I was in college in the North and took a course in Southern writers and the South. The perfection of her writing was so dazzling I never noticed that no black Southern writers were taught. The other writers we studied—Faulkner, McCullers, Welty—seemed obsessed with a racial past that would not let them go. They seemed to beg the question of their characters' humanity on every page. O'Connor's characters—whose humanity if not their sanity is taken for granted, and who are miserable, ugly, narrow-minded, atheistic, and of intense racial smugness and arrogance, with not a graceful, pretty one anywhere who is not, at the same time, a joke—shocked and delighted me.

It was for her description of Southern white women that I appreciated her work at first, because when she set her pen to them not a whiff of magnolia hovered in the air (and the tree itself might never have been planted), and yes, I could say, yes, these white folks without the magnolia (who are indifferent to the tree's existence), and these black folks without melons and superior racial patience, these are like Southerners that I know.

She was for me the first great modern writer from the South, and was, in any case, the only one I had read who wrote such sly, demythifying sentences about white women as: "The woman would be more or less pretty—yellow hair, fat ankles, muddy-colored eyes."

Her white male characters do not fare any better—all of them misfits, thieves, deformed madmen, idiot children, illiterates, and murderers, and her black characters, male and female appear equally shallow, demented, and absurd. That she retained a certain distance (only, however, in her later, mature work) from the inner workings of her black characters seems to me all to her credit, since, by deliberately limiting her treatment of them to cover their observable demeanor and actions, she leaves them free, in the reader's imagination, to inhabit another landscape, another life, than the one she creates for them. This is a kind of grace many writers do not have when dealing with representatives of an oppressed people within a story, and their insistence on knowing everything, on being God, in fact, has burdened us with more stereotypes than we can ever hope to shed.

In her life, O'Connor was more casual. In a letter to her friend Robert Fitzgerald in the mid-fifties she wrote, "as the niggers say, I have the misery." He found nothing offensive, apparently, in including this unflattering (to O'Connor) statement in his Introduction to one of her books. O'Connor was then certain she was dying, and was in pain; one assumes she made this comment in an attempt at levity. Even so, I do not find it funny. In another letter she wrote shortly before she died she said: "Justice is justice and should not be appealed to along racial lines. The problem is not abstract for the Southerner, it's concrete: he sees it in terms of persons, not races—which way of seeing does away with easy answers." Of course this observation, though grand, does not apply to the racist treatment of blacks by whites in the South, and O'Connor should have added that she spoke only for herself.

But *essential* O'Connor is not about race at all, which is why it is so refreshing, coming, as it does, out of such a *racial* culture. If it can be said to be "about" anything, then it is "about" prophets and prophecy, "about" revelation, and "about" the impact of supernatural grace on human beings who don't have a chance of spiritual growth without it.

An indication that *she* believed in justice for the individual (if only in the corrected portrayal of a character she invented) is shown by her endless reworking of "The Geranium," the first story she published (in 1946), when she was twenty-one. She revised the story several times, renamed it at least twice, until, nearly twenty years after she'd originally published it (and significantly, I think, after the beginning of the Civil Rights Movement), it became a different tale. Her two main black characters, a man and a woman, underwent complete metamorphosis.

In the original story, Old Dudley, a senile racist from the South, lives with his daughter in a New York City building that has "niggers" living in it too. The black characters are described as being passive, self-effacing people. The black woman sits quietly, hands folded, in her apartment; the man, her husband, helps Old Dudley up the stairs when the old man is out of breath, and chats with him kindly, if condescendingly, about guns and hunting. But in the final version of the story, the woman walks around Old

Dudley (now called Tanner) as if he's an open bag of garbage, scowls when-ever she sees him, and "didn't look like any kind of woman, black or white, he had ever seen." Her husband, whom Old Dudley persists in calling "Preacher" (under the misguided assumption that to all black men it is a courtesy title), twice knocks the old man down. At the end of the story he stuffs Old Dudley's head, arms, and legs through the banisters of the stair-way "as if in a stockade," and leaves him to die. The story's final title is "Judgment Day."

The quality added is rage, and, in this instance, O'Connor waited until she saw it *exhibited* by black people before she recorded it.

She was an artist who thought she might die young, and who then knew for certain she would. Her view of her characters pierces right through to the skull. Whatever her characters' color or social position she saw them as she saw herself, in the light of imminent mortality. Some of her stories, "The Enduring Chill" and "The Comforts of Home" especially, seem to be writ-ten out of the despair that must, on occasion, have come from this bleak vision, but it is for her humor that she is most enjoyed and remembered. My favorites are these:

> Everywhere I go I'm asked if I think the universities stifle writers. My opinion is that they don't stifle enough of them. There's many a best-seller that could have been prevented by a good teacher.
>
> —*Mystery and Manners*

> "She would of been a good woman, if it had been somebody there to shoot her every minute of her life."
>
> —*A Good Man Is Hard To Find*

> There are certain cases in which, if you can only learn to write poorly enough, you can make a great deal of money.
>
> —*Mystery and Manners*

> It is the business of fiction to embody mystery through manners, and mystery is a great embarrassment to the modern mind.
>
> —*Mystery and Manners*

It mattered to her that she was a Catholic. This comes as a surprise to those who first read her work as that of an atheist. She believed in all the mysteries of her faith. And yet, she was incapable of writing dogmatic or formulaic stories. No religious facts, nothing haloed softly in celestial light, not even any happy endings. It has puzzled some of her readers and annoyed the Catholic church that in her stories not only does good not triumph, it is not usually present. Seldom are there choices, and God never intervenes to help anyone win. To O'Connor, in fact, Jesus was God, and he won only by losing. She perceived that not much has been learned by his death by crucifixion, and that it is only by his continual, repeated dying—touching one's own life in a direct, searing way—that the meaning of that original loss is pressed into the heart of the individual.

In "The Displaced Person," a story published in 1954, a refugee from Poland is hired to work on a woman's dairy farm. Although he speaks in apparent gibberish, he is a perfect worker. He works so assiduously the woman begins to prosper beyond her greatest hopes. Still, because his ways are not her own (the Displaced Person attempts to get one of the black dairy workers to marry his niece by "buying" her out of a Polish concentration camp), the woman allows a runaway tractor to roll over and kill him.

"As far as I'm concerned," she tells the priest, "Christ was just another D.P." He just didn't fit in. After the death of the Polish refugee, however, she understands her complicity in a modern crucifixion, and recognizes the enormity of her responsibility for other human beings. The impact of this new awareness debilitates her; she loses her health, her farm, even her ability to speak.

This moment of revelation, when the individual comes face to face with her own limitations and comprehends "the true frontiers of her own inner country," is classic O'Connor, and always arrives in times of extreme crisis and loss.

There is a resistance by some to read O'Connor because she is "too difficult," or because they do not share her religious "persuasion." A young man who studied O'Connor under the direction of Eudora Welty some years ago amused me with the following story, which may or may not be true:

"I don't think Welty and O'Connor understood each *other*," he said, when I asked if he thought O'Connor would have liked or understood Welty's more conventional art. "For Welty's part, wherever we reached a particularly dense and symbolic section of one of O'Connor's stories she would sigh and ask, 'Is there a Catholic in the class?'"

Whether one "understands" her stories or not, one knows her characters are new and wondrous creations in the world and that not one of her stories—not even the earliest ones in which her consciousness of racial matters had not evolved sufficiently to be interesting or to differ much from the insulting and ignorant racial stereotyping that preceded it—could have been written by anyone else. As one can tell a Bearden from a Keene or a Picasso from a Hallmark card, one can tell an O'Connor story from any story laid next to it. Her Catholicism did not in any way limit (by defining it) her art. After her great stories of sin, damnation, prophecy, and revelation, the stories one reads casually in the average magazine seem to be about love and roast beef.

Andalusia is a large white house at the top of a hill with a view of a lake from its screened-in front porch. It is neatly kept, and there are, indeed, peacocks strutting about in the sun. Behind it there is an unpainted house where black people must have lived. It was, then, the typical middle-to-upper-class arrangement: white folks up front, the "help," in a far shabbier house, within calling distance from the back door. Although an acquaintance of O'Connor's has told me no one lives there now—but that a caretaker looks after things—I go up to the porch and knock. It is not an entirely empty or symbolic gesture: I have come to this vacant house to learn something about myself in relation to Flannery O'Connor, and will learn it whether anyone is home or not.

What I feel at the moment of knocking is fury that someone is paid to take care of her house, though no one lives in it and that her house still, in fact, stands, while mine—which of course we never owned anyway—is slowly rotting into dust. Her house becomes—in an instant—the symbol of my own disinheritance, and for that instant I hate her guts. All that she has meant to me is diminished, though her diminishment within me is against my will.

In Faulkner's backyard there is also an unpainted shack and a black caretaker still lives there, a quiet, somber man who, when asked about Faulkner's legendary "sense of humor" replied that, as far as he knew, "Mr. Bill never joked." For years while reading Faulkner, this image of the quiet man in the backyard shack stretched itself across the page.

Standing there knocking on Flannery O'Connor's door, I do not think of her illness, her magnificent work in spite of it; I think: it all comes back to houses. To how people live. There are rich people who own houses to live in and poor people who do not. And this is wrong. Literary separatism, fashionable now among blacks as it has always been among whites, is easier to practice than to change a fact like this. I think: I would level this country with the sweep of my hand, if I could.

"Nobody can change the past," says my mother.

"Which is why revolutions exist," I reply.

My bitterness comes from a deeper source than my knowledge of the difference, historically, race has made in the lives of white and black artists. The fact that in Mississippi no one even remembers where Richard Wright lived, while Faulkner's house is maintained by a black caretaker is painful, but not unbearable. What comes close to being unbearable is that I know how damaging to my own psyche such injustice is. In an unjust society the soul of the sensitive person is in danger of deformity from just such weights as this. For a long time I will feel Faulkner's house, O'Connor's house, crushing me. To fight back will require a certain amount of energy, energy better used doing something else.

My mother has been busy reasoning that, since Flannery O'Connor died young of a lingering and painful illness, the hand of God has shown itself. Then she sighs. "Well, you know," she says, "it is true, as they say, that the grass is always greener on the other side. That is, until you find yourself over there."

In a just society, of course, clichés like this could not survive.

But grass *can* be greener on the other side and not be just an illusion," I say. "Grass on the other side of the fence might have good fertilizer, while grass on your side might have to grow, if it grows at all, in sand."

We walk about quietly, listening to the soft sweep of the peacocks' tails as they move across the yard. I notice how completely O'Connor, in her fiction, has described just this view of the rounded hills, the tree line, black against the sky, the dirt road that runs from the front yard down to the highway. I remind myself of her courage and of how much—in her art—she has helped me to see. She destroyed the last vestiges of sentimentality in white Southern writing; she caused white women to look ridiculous on pedestals, and she approached her black characters—as a mature artist—with unusual humility and restraint. She also cast spells and worked magic with the written word. The magic, the wit, and the mystery of Flannery O'Connor I know I will always love, I also know the meaning of the expression "Take what you can use and let the rest rot." If ever there was an expression designed to protect the health of the spirit, this is it.

As we leave O'Connor's yard the peacocks—who she said would have the last word—lift their splendid tails for our edification. One peacock is so involved in the presentation of his masterpiece he does not allow us to move the car until he finishes with his show.

"Peacocks are inspiring," I say to my mother, who does not seem at all in awe of them and actually frowns when she sees them strut, "but they sure don't stop to consider they might be standing in your way."

And she says, "Yes, and they'll eat up every bloom you have, if you don't watch out."

EDDIE GREEN

A GOOD MAN
IS HARD TO FIND*

My heart's sad and I am all for-lorn, My man's treating me mean.
I regret the day that I was born. And that man of mine I've ever seen.
My happiness, it never lasts a day, My heart is almost breaking while I say:

A GOOD MAN IS HARD TO FIND;
You always get the other kind.
Just when you think that he is your pal.
You look for him and find him fooling 'round some other gal.
Then you rave, you even crave, To see him laying in his grave.
So if your man is nice, take my advice
And hug him in the morning, Kiss him ev'ry night,
Give him plenty lovin', Treat him right,
For a good man now-a-days Is hard to find.

Yesterday my heart from care was free, I sang all through the day.
Now the blues have overtaken me, Since my lovin' man has gone away.
I tried my best to treat him nice and kind,
But now these words are running through my mind:

A GOOD MAN IS HARD TO FIND;
You always get the other kind.
Just when you think that he is your pal.
You look for him and find him fooling 'round some other gal.
Then you rave, you even crave, To see him laying in his grave.
So if your man is nice, take my advice
And hug him in the morning, Kiss him ev'ry night,
Give him plenty lovin', Treat him right,
For a good man now-a-days Is hard to find.

*This famous blues song, copyright 1917, was written by Eddie Green and made popular by Bessie Smith, as well as other singers.

Sample Student Research Paper

Renae Martin
Professor Zaidman
Composition and Literature
June 24, 1999

Sin and Punishment
According to Flannery O'Connor

In "A Good Man Is Hard to Find" Flannery
O'Connor presents a religious dualism—the grandmother who deems herself worthy of salvation and
The Misfit who questions the justice of God. The
grandmother is a deceptive, manipulative woman
who lies and uses her grandchildren to dominate
and manipulate her son to get what she wants. Her
attempt to gain control over The Misfit in the
same manner she uses with her family backfires
when he confronts her with his questions about
good versus evil and about belief in Christ.

Whereas grandmothers are usually associated
with love, kindness, and virtue, O'Connor's
grandmother is a manipulative, domineering woman
who talks too much for her and her family's own
good. Her greatest success in manipulation occurs
when she entices the children with the story of
the "nearby" plantation house. She wants to see
it again, but lets the children—with their kick-
ing and screaming—convince Bailey to turn off
the main road to go in search of the house. "She
uses language for her own purposes, trying to

(right margin annotations)

Introduction
presents the story's
main conflict

Thesis statement

Analysis of the
grandmother's
manipulative
behavior

Martin 2

manipulate her son and the Misfit in order to assume superiority over them" (Highsmith p. 80). It is she who signs the family's death warrant with her own tongue. She is the instigator of the children's demand to turn off the main road to find the plantation house. And it is she who, with her recognition of The Misfit, seals their fate: "'it would have been better for all of you, lady, if you hadn't of reckernized me,'" (p. 29) he says after she blurts out his identity.

The grandmother, much like the devil, is sneaky. Like the serpent in the Garden of Eden, she is wily and crafty. Because the grandmother manipulates them into doing what she wants, "the family's predicament traces directly to the old woman's selfishness and stupidity" (Coulthard p. 71). She would have been wise to bear in mind Proverbs 10:19: "When words are many, sin is not absent, but he who holds his tongue is wise." With her manipulations and the children's tirades, Bailey gives in to their demands to see the plantation house. Thus, the grandmother's words ultimately lead to the death of her and her family.

Critic used to support interpretation

Even her son Bailey cannot save her. Although he lives up to society's expectations by allowing his mother to live with his family, they do not share a close relationship. Interestingly, a bailey is a castle's outer wall meant to ward off potential attackers, and Bailey has built an

Analysis continues with Bailey, followed by the rest of the family in subsequent paragraphs

Martin 3

emotional wall around himself in an effort to
block out his mother. As she tries to speak to
him, he ignores her and does not even look up
from reading the newspaper. Perhaps he does this
to protect himself from his mother's manipulations. The irony of his name becomes apparent
later when the cold-blooded killers confront his
family, and Bailey can do nothing to protect them
or himself because he is powerless in the situation he has allowed his family to get him into.

By not giving names to the mother or the
baby, O'Connor shows their insignificance to
their family and the story. They are, in essence,
so unimportant to the outcome of the story that
they receive only passing reference. The mother's
function in the story lies in the fact that John
Wesley and June Star need a mother in this traditional 1950s family. She provides a contrast
to the grandmother, who, dressed in a prim and
proper manner for the trip, wants everyone to
understand immediately that she is a lady. However, the children's mother is almost comical,
wearing "a green headkerchief that had two points
on the top like rabbit's ears" and has a face re-
sembling a cabbage (p. 21). It is hard to respect
someone who looks like a vegetable. The baby's
purpose is to show how cold-hearted The Misfit
and his gang are, because they would take an
innocent life without a qualm.

Quoted description
shows humor

Martin 4

As for the other two children, their behavior
contradicts their names. John Wesley runs counter
to the character of his namesake, John Wesley
(1703-91), founder of Methodism, and June Star
conjures up neither June's warmth or sunshine nor
a twinkling heavenly body. The children behave
wildly, rudely, and obnoxiously in the car and
the restaurant and make comments such as "'If
you don't want to go to Florida, why dontcha
stay at home?'" (p. 21) and "'I wouldn't live
in a broken down place like this for a million
bucks!'" Even when faced with the guns of The
Misfit and his men, June Star finds it impossible
to hold her tongue. She refuses to hold hands
with Bobby Lee because she thinks he looks like
a pig. With their father closed off and their
mother insignificant, it is easy to see how they
have modeled themselves after their grandmother
in their outspoken, manipulative ways.

Quoted dialogue illustrates characterization

To The Misfit, the family is nothing more
than a complication. They mean nothing to him
other than the fact that they are witnesses. In
his distorted thinking, their deaths would not
lie heavily on his conscience since he does not
directly tell his underlings Hiram and Bobby
Lee to kill them, nor does he see them do it.
However, killing the grandmother is personal.
He feels she should be punished for her own mis-
deeds. "He faces himself and his actions squarely

Martin 5

and demands that the grandmother do the same"
(Highsmith p. 80). Maybe the family would have
lived if the grandmother had not said she recognized The Misfit, or maybe they would have died
regardless.

The Misfit is self-named, and his name has
multiple meanings. His own reason for calling
himself The Misfit is simple: "'I can't make what
all I done wrong fit what all I gone through
in punishment'" (p. 33). The punishment misfits
the crime. Literally, his clothes misfit as
well: "The Misfit's 'borrowed' blue jeans are
too tight" (Tate p. 93). Another definition that
describes O'Connor's character is one who is
poorly adjusted to the environment. The Misfit
states, "'My daddy said I was a different breed
of dog . . .'" (p. 31). Perhaps he has a mental
illness that has shaken his faith because he
finds it hard to understand why God would afflict
him. Whatever his ailment, he does not believe he
has been treated fairly by either God or secular
authorities. This is confirmed by a question he
poses to the grandmother: "'Does it seem right
to you, lady, that one is punished a heap and
another ain't punished at all'" (p. 33)?

The Misfit seeks a certainty of salvation.
This leads him on the same path followed by
Martin Luther (1483-1546) and John Calvin (1509-
64) during the Protestant Reformation of the
sixteenth century. Luther's quest to reform the

Further character analysis

Lecture notes from History of Western Civilization course; no documentation necessary

Martin 6

Catholic Church centered on the concept of the
justice of God, a precondition to salvation in
which God weighs the merits of good works. Like
Luther, The Misfit believes weak humans could
never satisfy God on those terms alone. Luther
and Calvin both believed in the grace of God,
in which salvation was given freely through the
sacrifice of Christ. In I Timothy 1:12-16, the
Apostle Paul describes the Lord's grace, which
granted him salvation. The Misfit believes
Christ's "offer of salvation through grace has
also disturbed the balance of the scales of justice" (Bellamy p. 54). Luther saw justification
by faith as an all-important first step to salvation, while good works come second, stemming
from gratitude to God. The Misfit (like Luther
before him) has problems with his personal convictions that lead him to worry about the justice of God. He "sees the world in absolutes"
(Highsmith p. 81). By stating "'I can't make
what all I done wrong fit what all I gone through
in punishment" (p. 33), The Misfit is implying,
"there [is] no balance between guilt and punishment . . ." (Tate p. 95).

Another problem facing The Misfit is Calvin's
discussion of theology/concept of the total depravity of mankind. Original sin taints everything; no part of human life is immune from it.
Therefore, nothing one says, does, thinks, or
believes will be pure or strong enough for

Knowledge of the New Testament; no documentation necessary

Critic's views integrated into student's wording

Martin 7

justification. Only after God has bestowed His
grace is one capable of overcoming sin and
achieving salvation. The Misfit believes in predestination. God has already decided from the beginning who goes to Hell (the reprobate) and who
is saved (the elect). Humans are responsible inherently and individually for Original Sin and
cannot do anything to effect salvation (Bellamy
p. 52). So, what difference does it make what a
person does if the decision has already been
made? In fact, The Misfit fancies himself a sinner. Deserved justice for him would obviously
mean eternal damnation. Humans are, by nature,
weak, immoral, and sinful beings, so why not go
on "killing somebody or burning down his house or
doing some other meanness"? In other words, why
not make the crimes committed fit the ultimate
deserved punishment?

Paraphrase changes syntax and wording from the source

While talking to The Misfit, the grandmother
uses the term "good man" three times to try to
avert impending doom. What is her definition of
a "good man"? She calls Red Sammy Butts a "good
man" (p. 25). He owns his own business, The
Tower, and shares the grandmother's opinion that
there is a general lack of manners in the modern
world. Although not referred to as a "good man,"
Mr. Teagarden "was a gentleman" and "a very
wealthy man." Obviously, for her, the term implies wealth and class standing. To The Misfit
she lies, "I know you're a good man. You don't

Analysis of the title and theme of the story

look a bit like you have common blood". Here her manipulation of The Misfit backfires because he knows she is lying. "The story's moral point is carried by the grandmother, who is another of O'Connor's shallow, complacent women for whom appearance is the only reality" (Coulthard p. 71). The way she dresses for the trip, wanting to be seen as a lady, the female counterpart to a good man, reflects her viewpoint that appearance is everything. Her assumption is hypocritical, as shown by the Apostle Paul in I Timothy 2:9-10: "I also want women to dress modestly, with decency and propriety, not with braided hair or gold or pearls or expensive clothes, but with good deeds, appropriate for women who profess to worship God"—or Jesus Christ, the ultimate "good man."

In a last-ditch effort to save her life, the grandmother tells The Misfit, "'You've got good blood! I know you wouldn't shoot a lady'" (p. 33)! He recognizes she is not a lady and is most concerned with herself. When she realizes she cannot save her life by praising The Misfit, she tries to appeal to him by agreeing that "'maybe He [Christ] didn't raise the dead'" (p. 33). She has probably never given religion, God, or prayer any serious thought before her final moments, although she has always considered herself worthy of salvation by having others see her as a lady. The grandmother is "until

Martin 9

the moment of her death, a thorough hypocrite"
(Bellamy p. 53). For The Misfit, killing the
grandmother is justified as the ultimate punishment for her sins of manipulation, blasphemy, and
hypocrisy. Perhaps he feels that in killing her,
he is doing the world a favor by sending a mean
old woman to her final judgment. The only thing
that redeems the grandmother in the end is her
realization of being doomed, if not to Hell, then
to death. She knows that she is going to die no
matter what she tries to do to reverse that outcome. Her last
efforts to save her own life serve only to reinforce The Misfit's resolve to kill, or more
pointedly, to punish her for her sins. She does
manage to find salvation, however, when she falls
to her knees and then recognizes The Misfit as
one of her own children. "In accepting this miserable, lowly sinner as one of her own children,
this once proud lady is admitting to her own
sinful nature for the first time, and it is in
this epiphany that she finds salvation" (Coulthard p. 73).

Given these theological questions, this is
not a story of Catholic versus Protestant doctrine. The only character with even remote religious leanings appears to be The Misfit, and his
questions are Protestant in nature. He seems concerned with life but, unlike the grandmother, his
concern lies in spiritual life and salvation, not

Discussion of The
Misfit's motivation

Martin 10

physical life. The grandmother is not a medium
of grace for him but instead, a medium for him
to test the waters of God's justification, faith,
predestination, and ultimately, salvation. The
Misfit finds no goodness or "pleasure in life"
(p. 34) only the "meanness" (p. 33) he sees
within himself and the grandmother.

Conclusion
reinforces the thesis

Works Cited

Bellamy, Michael O. "Everything Off Balance: Protestant Election in Flannery O'Connor's 'A Good Man Is Hard to Find.'" Zaidman 50-56.

Bryant, Hallman B. "Reading the Map in 'A Good Man Is Hard to Find.'" Zaidman 56-62.

Coulthard, A. R. "Flannery O'Connor's Deadly Conversions." Zaidman 70-74.

Highsmith, Dixie Lee. "Flannery O'Connor's Polite Conversation." Zaidman 75-81.

The Holy Bible. New International Version. Grand Rapids, MI: Zondervan: 1978.

O'Connor, Flannery. "A Good Man Is Hard to Find." Zaidman 21-34.

Tate, J. O., Jr. "A Good Source Is Not So Hard to Find." Zaidman 92-95.

Zaidman, Laura Mandell, ed. "<u>A Good Man Is Hard to Find</u>." The Harcourt Brace Casebook Series in Literature. Fort Worth: Harcourt, 1999.

Bibliography

Works by Flannery O'Connor

FICTION AND NONFICTION COLLECTION

Flannery O'Connor: Collected Works. Ed. Sally Fitzgerald. New York: Library of
America, 1988

SHORT STORY COLLECTIONS

A Good Man Is Hard to Find. New York: Harcourt, 1955.
Everything That Rises Must Converge. Ed. Robert Fitzgerald. New York: Far-
rar, 1965.
The Complete Stories of Flannery O'Connor. New York: Farrar, 1971.

NOVELS

Wise Blood. New York: Harcourt, 1952.
The Violent Bear It Away. New York: Farrar, 1960.

ESSAYS AND BOOK REVIEWS

"The Church and the Fiction Writer." *America* 96 (30 Mar. 1957): 733–35.
"The Fiction Writer and His Country." *The Living Novel.* Ed. Granville Hicks.
New York: Macmillan, 1957. 157–64.
"Living with a Peacock." *Holiday* 30 (Sept. 1961): 52.
A Memoir of Mary Ann. Introduction. New York: Farrar, 1961.
Mystery and Manners: Occasional Prose. Ed. Sally and Robert Fitzgerald. New York:
Farrar, 1969.
The Presence of Grace and Other Book Reviews by Flannery O'Connor. Comp. Leo J.
Zuber. Ed. Carter W. Martin. Athens: U of Georgia P, 1983.
Rev. of *The Phenomenon of Man,* by Pierre Teilhard de Chardin. *American Scholar*
30 (Fall 1961): 618.
"The Regional Writer." *Esprit* 7 (Winter 1963): 32–55.
"Why Do the Heathens Rage?" *Esquire* 60 (July 1963): 60–61.

Letters

The Correspondence of Flannery O'Connor and the Brainard Cheneys. Ed. Charles
Ralph Stephens. Jackson: UP of Mississippi, 1986.
The Habit of Being: Letters of Flannery O'Connor. Ed. Sally Fitzgerald. New York:
Farrar, 1979.

Works about Flannery O'Connor

Biography, Profiles, and Interviews

Coles, Robert. *Flannery O'Connor's South.* Baton Rouge: Louisiana State UP, 1980.
Fitzgerald, Sally. Introduction. *The Habit of Being: Letters of Flannery O'Connor.*
New York: Farrar, 1979. ix–xvii.
Magee, Rosemary M., Ed. *Conversations with Flannery O'Connor.* Jackson: UP of
Mississippi, 1987.

Criticism and Commentary

Asals, Frederick. "The Aesthetics of Incongruity." *Flannery O'Connor: The Imagi-
nation of Extremity.* Athens: U of Georgia P, 1982. 142–154.
---, ed. *"A Good Man Is Hard to Find."* Women Writers: Text and Contexts ser.
New Brunswick, NJ: Rutgers UP, 1993.
Bacon, Jon Lance. *Flannery O'Connor and Cold War Culture.* Cambridge, England:
Cambridge UP, 1993.
Baumgaertner, Jill P. *Flannery O'Connor: A Proper Scaring.* Wheaton, IL: Harold
Shaw, 1988.
Beaver, Harold. "On the Verge of Eternity." *The [London] Times Literary Supple-
ment.* 4051 (21 Nov. 1980): 1336.
Bellamy, Michael O. "Everything Off Balance: Protestant Election in Flannery
O'Connor's 'A Good Man Is Hard to Find.'" *Flannery O'Connor Bulletin*
8 (1979): 116–24.
Bloom, Harold. Ed. *Flannery O'Connor: Modern Critical Views.* New York:
Chelsea, 1986.
Brinkmeyer, Robert H. Jr. *The Art and Vision of Flannery O'Connor.* Baton Rouge:
Louisiana State UP, 1989.
---. "Flannery O'Connor and the Demonic." *Modern Fiction Studies* Spring 1973:
29–41.
Browning, Preston M., Jr. *Flannery O'Connor.* Carbondale: Southern Illinois
UP, 1974.

Bryant, Hallman B. "Reading the Map in 'A Good Man Is Hard to Find.'" *Studies in Short Fiction* 18 (1981): 301–07.

Butler, Rebecca R. "What's So Funny About Flannery O'Connor?" *Flannery O'Connor Bulletin* 9 (1980): 30–40.

Butterworth, Nancy K. "Flannery O'Connor." *American Novelists Since World War II, Fourth Series.* Ed. James and Wanda Giles. *Dictionary of Literary Biography.* Vol. 152. Detroit: Gale, 1995. 158–81.

Cheney, Brainard. "Flannery O'Connor's Campaign for Her Country." *Sewanee Review* 72.4 (1964): 555–58.

---. "Miss O'Connor Creates Unusual Humor Out of Ordinary Sin." *Sewanee Review* 71 (Autumn 1963): 644–52.

Coffey, Warren. "Flannery O'Connor." *Commentary* 40.5 (Nov. 1965): 93–99.

Coulthard, A. R. "Flannery O'Connor's Deadly Conversions." *Flannery O'Connor Bulletin* 13 (1984): 87–98.

---. "From Sermon to Parable: Four Conversion Stories by Flannery O'Connor." *American Literature* 55.1 (1983): 55–71.

Desmond, John F. *Risen Sons: Flannery O'Connor's Vision of History.* Athens: U of Georgia P, 1987.

---. "Signs of the Times: Lancelot and The Misfit." *Flannery O'Connor Bulletin* 18 (1989): 91–98.

Dibble, Terry J. *Flannery O'Connor's Short Stories, Notes.* Lincoln, NE: Cliffs Notes, 1986.

Di Renzo, Anthony. *American Gargoyles: Flannery O'Connor and the Medieval Grotesque.* Carbondale: Southern Illinois UP, 1993.

Dowell, Bob. "The Moment of Grace in the Fiction of Flannery O'Connor." *College English* 27.3 (1965): 235–39.

Doxey, William S. "A Dissenting Opinion of Flannery O'Connor's 'A Good Man Is Hard to Find.'" *Studies in Short Fiction* 10 (Spring 1973): 199–204.

Drake, Robert. "The Bleeding Stinking Mad Shadow of Jesus in the Fiction of Flannery O'Connor." *Comparative Literature Studies* 3.2 (1966): 183–96.

---. *Flannery O'Connor: A Critical Essay.* Contemporary Writers in Christian Perspective ser. Grand Rapids, MI: Eerdmans, 1966.

---. "The Paradigm of Flannery O'Connor's True Country." *Studies in Short Fiction* 6.4 (1969): 433–42.

Driggers, Stephen G., Robert J. Dunn, and Sarah E. Gordon. *The Manuscripts of Flannery O'Connor at Georgia College.* Athens: U of Georgia P, 1989.

Driskell, Leon V., and Joan T. Brittain. *The Eternal Crossroads: The Art of Flannery O'Connor.* Lexington: UP of Kentucky, 1971.

Duhamel, P. Albert. "Flannery O'Connor's Violent View of Reality." *Catholic World* Feb. 1960: 280–85.

Dyson, J. Peter. "Cats, Crime, and Punishment: *The Mikado's* Pitti-Sing in 'A Good Man Is Hard to Find.'" *English Studies in Canada* 14 (1988): 436–52.

Edelstein, Mark G. "Flannery O'Connor and the Problem of Modern Satire." *Studies in Short Fiction* Spring 1975: 139–44.

Eggenschwiler, David. *The Christian Humanism of Flannery O'Connor.* Detroit: Wayne State UP, 1972.

Ellis, James. "Watermelons and Coca-Cola in 'A Good Man Is Hard to Find': Holy Communion in the South." *Notes on Contemporary Literature* 8 (1978): 7–8.

Ensor, Allison R. "Flannery O'Connor and Music." *Flannery O'Connor Bulletin* 14 (1985): 1–13.

Esprit 8.1 (Winter 1964). [A memorial issue devoted to O'Connor.]

Evans, Robert C. "Poe, O'Connor, and the Mystery of The Misfit." *Flannery O'Connor Bulletin* 25 (1996–97): 1–12.

Farnham, James F. "The Grotesque in Flannery O'Connor." *America* 105 (13 May 1961): 277–81.

Feeley, M. Kathleen. *Flannery O'Connor: Voice of the Peacock.* New Brunswick, NJ: Rutgers UP, 1972; New York: Fordham UP, 1982.

Fickett, Harold, and Douglas R. Gilbert. *Flannery O'Connor: Images of Grace.* Grand Rapids, MI: Eerdmans, 1986.

Fitzgerald, Robert. "The Countryside and the True Country." *Sewanee Review* 70 (Summer 1962): 380–94.

---. Introduction. *Everything That Rises Must Converge.* New York: Noonday, 1966. vii–xxxiv.

Friedman, Melvin J. "Flannery O'Connor: Another Legend in Southern Fiction." *English Journal* April 1962: 233–43. Reprinted in *Recent American Fiction: Some Critical Views.* Ed. Joseph J. Waldmeir. Boston: Houghton, 1963. 231–45.

Friedman, Melvin J., and Beverly Lyon Clark, eds. *Critical Essays on Flannery O'Connor.* Boston: Hall, 1985.

Friedman, Melvin J., and Lewis A. Lawson. *The Added Dimension: The Art and Mind of Flannery O'Connor.* New York: Fordham UP, 1977.

Gentry, Marshall Bruce. *Flannery O'Connor's Religion of the Grotesque.* Jackson: UP of Mississippi, 1986.

Getz, Lorine M. *Flannery O'Connor: Her Life, Library, and Book Reviews.* New York: Mellen, 1980.

---. *Nature and Grace in Flannery O'Connor's Fiction.* New York: Mellen, 1982.

Giannone, Richard. *Flannery O'Connor and the Mystery of Love.* Urbana: U of Illinois, 1989.

Gilman, Richard. "On Flannery O'Connor." *New York Review of Books* 13 (21 Aug. 1969): 24–26.

Giroux, Robert. Introduction. *The Complete Stories of Flannery O'Connor.* New York: Farrar, 1971. vii–xvii.

Golden, Robert E., and Mary C. Sullivan. *Flannery O'Connor and Caroline Gordon: A Reference Guide.* Boston: Hall, 1977.

Gordon, Caroline, et al. *Critique* 2.2 (1958). [articles on O'Connor by Gordon, Sister M. Bernetta Quinn, Louis D. Rubin, Jr., and George F. Wedge]

Gordon, Sarah. *Flannery O'Connor: The Obedient Imagination.* Athens: U of Georgia P [forthcoming].

---. "Maryat and Julian and the 'not so bloodless revolution.'" *Flannery O'Connor Bulletin* 21 (1992): 25–36.

Gossett, Louise Y. "The Test by Fire: Flannery O'Connor." *Violence in Recent Southern Fiction.* Durham, NC: Duke UP, 1965. 75–97.

Grimshaw, James A., Jr. *The Flannery O'Connor Companion.* Westport, CT: Greenwood, 1981.

Hamblen, Abigail Ann. "Flannery O'Connor's Study of Innocence and Evil." *University [of Missouri] Review* 34.4 (Summer 1968): 295–97.

Hardwick, Elizabeth. "Flannery O'Connor, 1925–1964." *New York Review of Books* 8 Oct. 1964: 21t.

Hart, Jane. "Strange Earth: The Stories of Flannery O'Connor." *Georgia Review* 12 (Summer 1958): 215–22.

Hawkes, John. "Flannery O'Connor's Devil." *Sewanee Review* Summer 1962: 395–407.

Hawkins, Peter S. *The Language of Grace: Flannery O'Connor, Walker Percy, and Iris Murdoch.* Cambridge, MA: Cowley, 1983.

Hendin, Josephine. *The World of Flannery O'Connor.* Bloomington: Indiana UP, 1970.

Hicks, Granville. "A Cold, Hard Look at Humankind." *Saturday Review* 48 (29 May 1965): 22–23.

---. "A Writer at Home with Her Heritage." *Saturday Review* 45 (12 May 1962): 22–23.

Highsmith, Dixie Lee. "Flannery O'Connor's Polite Conversation." *Flannery O'Connor Bulletin* 11 (1982): 94–107

Hoffman, Frederick J. "James Agee and Flannery O'Connor: The Religious Consciousness." *The Art of Southern Fiction: A Study of Some Modern Novelists.* Carbondale: Southern Illinois P, 1967.

Howe, Irving. "Flannery O'Connor's Stories." *New York Review of Books* 30 Sept. 1965: 16–17.

Humphries, Jefferson. *The Otherness Within: Gnostic Readings in Marcel Proust, Flannery O'Connor, and Francois Villon.* Baton Rouge: Louisiana State UP, 1983.

Hyman, Stanley Edgar. "Flannery O'Connor." *Seven American Women Writers of the Twentieth Century: An Introduction.* Ed. Maureen Howard. Minneapolis: U of Minnesota P, 1977. 311–55.

Idol, John. Rev. of *The Complete Stories. Studies in Short Fiction* Winter 1973: 103–04.

Johansen, Ruthann Knechel. *The Narrative Secret of Flannery O'Connor.* Tuscaloosa: U of Alabama P, 1994.

Jones, Madison. "A Good Man's Predicament." *Southern Review* 20 (1984): 836–41.

Katz, Claire. "Flannery O'Connor's Rage of Vision." *American Literature* Mar. 1974: 54–67.

Kessler, Edward. *Flannery O'Connor and the Language of Apocalypse.* Princeton, NJ: Princeton UP, 1986.

Kinney, Arthur F. *Flannery O'Connor's Library: Resources of Being.* Athens: U of Georgia P, 1985.

Kropf, C. R. "Theme and Setting in 'A Good Man Is Hard to Find.'" *Renascence* 24 (1972): 177t.

Lasseter, Victor. "The Children's Names in Flannery O'Connor's 'A Good Man Is Hard to Find.'" *Notes on Modern American Literature* 6 (1982): item 6.

---. "The Genesis of Flannery O'Connor's 'A Good Man Is Hard to Find.'" *Studies in American Fiction* 10 (1982): 227–32.

Lee, Hermione. "Resigned to Death." *New Statesman* 98 (7 Dec. 1979): 895–96.

Logsdon, Loren, and Charles W. Mayer, eds. *Since Flannery O'Connor: Essays on the Contemporary American Short Story.* Essays in Literature ser. Macomb, IL: Western Illinois UP, 1987.

McCown, Robert. "Flannery O'Connor and the Reality of Sin." *Catholic World* 188 (Jan. 1959): 285–91.

McFarland, Dorothy Tuck. *Flannery O'Connor.* Modern Literature Monographs ser. New York: Ungar, 1976.

McKenzie, Barbara. *Flannery O'Connor's Georgia.* Athens: U of Georgia P, 1980.

McMullen, Joanne Halleran. *Writing against God: Language as Message in the Literature of Flannery O'Connor.* Macon, GA: Mercer UP, 1996.

Maida, Patricia D. "Light and Enlightenment in Flannery O'Connor's Fiction." *Studies in Short Fiction* 14 (1976): 31–36.

Maloff, Saul. "On Flannery O'Connor." *Commonweal* 8 Aug. 1969: 490–91.

Marks, W. S., III. "Advertisements for Grace: Flannery O'Connor's 'A Good Man Is Hard to Find.'" *Studies in Short Fiction* 4 (1966): 19–27.

Martin, Carter W. "'The Meanest of Them Sparkled': Beauty and Landscape in Flannery O'Connor's Fiction." *Realist of Distances: Flannery O'Connor Revisited.* Ed. Karl-Heinz Westarp and Jan Nordby Gretlund. Aarhus, Denmark: Aarhus UP, 1987.

---. *The True Country: Themes in the Fiction of Flannery O'Connor.* Nashville: Vanderbilt UP, 1969.

May, John R. "Flannery O'Connor." *American Novelists Since World War II.* Ed. Jeffrey Helterman and Richard Layman. *Dictionary of Literary Biography.* Vol. 2. Detroit: Gale, 1978. 383–87.

---. "Flannery O'Connor." *The New Consciousness, 1941–1968. Concise Dictionary of American Literary Biography.* Detroit: Gale, 1987. 399–407.

---. *The Pruning Word: The Parables of Flannery O'Connor.* Notre Dame: U of Notre Dame P, 1976.

Milder, Robert. "The Protestantism of Flannery O'Connor." *Southern Review* 11 (1975): 802–19.

Montgomery, Marion. *Why Flannery O'Connor Stayed Home.* La Salle: Sherwood Sugden, 1981.

Muller, Gilbert H. *Nightmares and Visions: Flannery O'Connor and the Catholic Grotesque.* Athens: U of Georgia P, 1972.

Oates, Joyce Carol. "Realism of Distance, Realism of Immediacy." *Southern Review* 7 (1971): 295–313.

Orvell, Miles. *Invisible Parade: The Fiction of Flannery O'Connor.* Philadelphia: Temple UP, 1972. [Reprinted, with revised preface, as *Flannery O'Connor: An Introduction.* Jackson: UP of Mississippi, 1991.]

Paulson, Suzanne Morrow. *Flannery O'Connor: A Study of the Short Fiction.* Boston: Twayne, 1988.

Pearson, Michael. *Imagined Places: Journeys into Literary America.* Jackson: UP of Mississippi, 1991.

Portch, Stephen R. *Literature's Silent Language: A Study of the Short Fiction.* New York: Lang, 1985.

---.. "O'Connor's 'A Good Man Is Hard to Find.'" *Explicator* 37.1 (1978): 19–20.

Quinn, John J. *Flannery O'Connor: A Memorial.* Scranton: U of Scranton P, 1995.

---. "A Reading of Flannery O'Connor." *Thought* 48 (1973): 520–31.

Ragen, Brian Abel. *A Wreck on the Road to Damascus: Innocence, Guilt, and Conversion in Flannery O'Connor.* Chicago: Loyola UP, 1989.

Rath, Sura P., and Mary Neff Shaw. *Flannery O'Connor: New Perspectives.* Athens: U of Georgia P, 1996.

Reiter, Robert E., ed. *Flannery O'Connor.* St. Louis: Herder, 1968.

Renner, Stanley. "Secular Meaning in 'A Good Man Is Hard to Find.'" *College Literature* 9 (1982): 123–32.

Rose Alice [Sister]. "Flannery O'Connor: Poet to the Outcast." *Renascence* 16 (1964): 126–32.

Rowse, A. L. "Flannery O'Connor—Genius of the South." *Books and Bookmen* May 1972: 38–39.

Schaub, Thomas Hill. "Christian Realism and O'Connor's *A Good Man Is Hard to Find.*" *American Fiction in the Cold War.* Madison: U of Wisconsin P, 1991. 116–36.

Scheick, William J. "Flannery O'Connor's 'A Good Man Is Hard to Find' and G. K. Chesterton's *Manalive.*" *Studies in American Fiction* 11 (1983): 241–45.

Schenck, Mary Jane. "Deconstructed Meaning in Two Short Stories by Flannery O'Connor." *Ambiguities in Literature and Film.* Ed. Hans P. Braendlin. Tallahassee: Florida State UP, 1988. 125–35.

Shloss, Carol. *Flannery O'Connor's Dark Comedies: The Limits of Inference.* Baton Rouge: Louisiana State UP, 1980.

Spivey, Ted R. *Flannery O'Connor: The Woman, the Thinker, the Visionary.* Macon, GA: Mercer UP, 1995.

---. "Flannery O'Connor's View of God and Man." *Studies in Short Fiction 1* 1964: 200-06.

Stephens, Martha. *The Question of Flannery O'Connor.* Baton Rouge: Louisiana State UP, 1973.

Sullivan, Walter. "The Achievement of Flannery O'Connor." *Southern Humanities Review* 2.3 (1968): 303–09.

---. *Death by Melancholy: Essays on Modern Southern Fiction.* Baton Rouge: Louisiana State UP, 1973.

Sweet-Hurd, Evelyn. "Finding O'Connor's Good Man." *Notes on Contemporary Literature* 14 (1984): 9–10.

Tate, J. O. Jr. "A Good Source Is Not So Hard to Find." *Flannery O'Connor Bulletin* 9 (1980): 98–103.

Thompson, Terry. "Doodlebug, Doodlebug: The Misfit in 'A Good Man Is Hard to Find.'" *Notes on Contemporary Literature* 17 (1987): 8–9.

---. "The Killers in O'Connor's 'A Good Man Is Hard to Find.'" *Notes on Contemporary Literature* 16 (1986): 4.

Walker, Alice. "Beyond the Peacock: The Reconstruction of Flannery O'Connor." *In Search of Our Mothers' Gardens: Womanist Prose.* San Diego: Harcourt, 1984. 42–59.

Walls, Doyle W. "O'Connor's 'A Good Man Is Hard to Find.'" *Explicator* 46 (Winter 1988): 43–45.

Walters, Dorothy. *Flannery O'Connor.* New York: Twayne, 1973.

Westarp, Karl-Heinz, and Jan Nordby Gretlund, eds. *Realist of Distances: Flannery O'Connor Revisited.* Aarhus, Denmark: Aarhus UP, 1987.

Westling, Louise. *Sacred Groves and Ravaged Gardens: The Fiction of Eudora Welty, Carson McCullers, and Flannery O'Connor.* Athens: U of Georgia P, 1985.

Whitt, Margaret Earley. *Understanding Flannery O'Connor.* Columbia: U of South Carolina P, 1995.

Williams, Melvin. "Black and White: A Study in Flannery O'Connor's Characters." *Black American Literature Forum* 10 (1976): 130–32.

Wood, Ralph C. *The Comedy of Redemption: Christian Faith and Comic Vision in Four American Novelists.* Notre Dame: U of Notre Dame P, 1988.

---. "Where Is the Voice Coming From? Flannery O'Connor on Race." *Flannery O'Connor Bulletin* 22 (1993–94): 90–118.

Woodward, Robert H. "A Good Route Is Hard to Find: Place Names and Setting in O'Connor's 'A Good Man Is Hard to Find.'" *Notes on Contemporary Literature* 3 (1973): 2–6.

Zaidman, Laura M. "Varieties of Religious Experience in O'Connor and West." *Flannery O'Connor Bulletin* 7 (1978): 26–46.

Journal

Gordon, Sarah, et al., eds. *Flannery O'Connor Bulletin*. Milledgeville: Georgia College & State University, 1972-present. [See *Flannery O'Connor Bulletin Index* for articles 1972–86, volumes 1–15]

Electronic and Other Media

Film and Video

"*Circle in the Fire*." Perf. Betty Miller and Katherine Miller. Perspective Films, 1976.

"*The Comforts of Home*." Dir. Jerome Shore. Phoenix/BFA Films & Video, 1974.

"*The Displaced Person*." Dir. Glenn Jordan. Perf. Irene Worth, John Houseman, Samuel L. Jackson, Shirley Stoler. Coronet, The Multimedia Co., 1977.

"*Good Country People*." Dir. Jeff Jackson. Perf. Johnnie Collins III, Shirley Slater, June Whitley Taylor, and Sue Marrow. Valley Video, ND.

"*The River*." Dir. Barbara Noble. The American Film Institute, 1976.

Wise Blood. Dir. John Huston. Perf. Brad Dourif, Ned Beatty, Harry Dean Stanton, Amy Wright, John Huston, and Daniel Shor. MCA/Universal Home Video, 1979.

Sound Recordings

A tape of O'Connor's reading of "A Good Man Is Hard To Find" at Vanderbilt University in April 1959—along with tapes of other speeches, readings, and interviews—is available at the Flannery O'Connor Collection in the Ina Dillard Russell Library at Georgia College & State University in Milledgeville. The Collection also has audiocassette tapes of papers presented at Flannery O'Connor Symposium sessions in 1977 and 1984. See the Web site for the Flannery O'Connor Collection under Internet Sources. Films and tapes are available at Georgia College & State University.

Internet Sources

General sources:

<http://ruby.ils.unc.edu/flannery/Bionotes.htm>.
<http://www.it.armstrong.edu/Academia/Schools/ArtScience/LLDA/
flannery/oconnor.txt>.
The Flannery O'Connor Special Collection:
<http://library.gcsu.edu/~sc/foc.htm/>.

Flannery O'Connor criticism: <scinfo@mail.gcsu.edu>.

Flannery O'Connor films and tapes: <http://library.gcsu.edu/~sc/focfilm.html>.

Flannery O'Connor Forum: Flannery-L (a scholarly electronic discussion group) focuses on O'Connor's life and writings. Postings include queries, discussion, conference announcements, information on new publications, and other topics relevant to O'Connor studies. An archive is updated periodically. Subscribe by sending an e-mail message (Subscribe) to <flannery-l@grumpy.gac.peachnet.edu>.

Essays on O'Connor:

Collum, Danny Duncan. "Nature and Grace: Flannery O'Connor and the Healing of Southern Culture."
<http://www2.ari.net/home/bsabath/941214.html>.

Helmer, Shane. "Stumbling onto the Spirit's Signposts."
<http://www2.ari.net/home/bsabath/941212.html>.

Mitchell, Jason P. "Tin Jesus: The Intellectual in Selected Short Fiction of Flannery O'Connor." <http://sunset.backbone.olemiss.edu/~jmitchel/flannery.htm>.

Polter, Julie. "Obliged to See God."
<http://www2.ari.net/home/bsabath/941211.html>.

Walker, Alice. "A South Without Myths."
<http://www2.ari.net/home/bsabath/941213.html>

Bibliography

Farmer, David. *Flannery O'Connor: A Descriptive Bibliography.* New York: Garland, 1981.

Appendix:
Documenting Sources

A Guide to MLA Documentation Style

Documentation is the acknowledgment of information from an outside source that you use in a paper. In general, you should give credit to your sources whenever you quote, paraphrase, summarize, or in any other way incorporate borrowed information or ideas into your work. Not to do so— on purpose or by accident—is to commit **plagiarism,** to appropriate the intellectual property of others. By following accepted conventions of documentation, you not only help avoid plagiarism, but also show your readers that you write with care and precision. In addition, you enable them to distinguish your ideas from those of your sources and, if they wish, to locate and consult the sources you cite.

Not all ideas from your sources need to be documented. You can assume that certain information—facts from encyclopedias, textbooks, newspapers, magazines, and dictionaries, or even from television and radio—is common knowledge. Even if the information is new to you, it need not be documented as long as it is found in several reference sources and as long as you do not use the exact wording of your source. Information that is in dispute or that is the original contribution of a particular person, however, *must* be documented. You need not, for example, document the fact that Arthur Miller's *Death of a Salesman* was first performed in 1949 or that it won a Pulitzer Prize for drama. (You could find this information in any current encyclopedia.) You would, however, have to document a critic's interpretation of a performance or a scholar's analysis of an early draft of the play, even if you do not use your source's exact words.

Students of literature use the documentation style recommended by the Modern Language Association of America (MLA), a professional organization of teachers and students of English and other languages. This method of documentation, the one that you should use any time you write a literature paper, has three components: *parenthetical references in the text, a list of works cited,* and *sometimes explanatory notes.*

Parenthetical References in the Text

MLA documentation uses references inserted in parentheses within the text that refer to an alphabetical list of works cited at the end of the paper. A typical **parenthetical reference** consists of the author's last name and a page number.

> Gwendolyn Brooks uses the sonnet form to create poems that have a wide social and aesthetic range (Williams 972).

If you use more than one source by the same author, include a shortened title in the parenthetical reference. In the following entry, "Brooks's Way" is a shortened form of the complete title of the article "Gwendolyn Brooks's Way with the Sonnet."

> Brooks not only knows Shakespeare, Spenser, and Milton, but she also knows the full range of African-American poetry (Williams, "Brooks's Way" 972).

If you mention the author's name or the title of the work in your paper, only a page reference is necessary.

> According to Gladys Margaret Williams in "Gwendolyn Brooks's Way with the Sonnet," Brooks combines a sensitivity to poetic forms with a depth of emotion appropriate for her subject matter (972-73).

Keep in mind that you use different punctuation for parenthetical references used with *paraphrases and summaries,* with *direct quotations run in with the text,* and with *quotations of more than four lines.*

Paraphrases and Summaries

Place the parenthetical reference after the last word of the sentence and before the final punctuation:

> In her works Brooks combines the pessimism of Modernist poetry with the optimism of the Harlem Renaissance (Smith 978).

Direct quotations run in with the text

Place the parenthetical reference after the quotation marks and before the final punctuation:

> According to Gary Smith, Brooks's <u>A Street in Bronzeville</u> "conveys the primacy of suffering in the lives of poor Black women" (980).

> According to Gary Smith, the poems in <u>A Street in Bronzeville</u> "served notice that Brooks had learned her craft . . ." (978).

> Along with Thompson we must ask, "Why did it take so long for critics to acknowledge that Gwendolyn Brooks is an important voice in twentieth-century American poetry?" (123)

Quotations set off from the text

Double-space above and below the quotation, as well as within the quotation. Quotations of more than four lines are indented ten spaces (or one inch) from the margin and are not enclosed within quotation marks. The first line of a single paragraph of quoted material is not indented further. If you quote two or more paragraphs, indent the first line of each paragraph three additional spaces (one-quarter inch).

Omit the quotation marks and place the parenthetical reference one space after the final punctuation.

> For Gary Smith, the identity of Brooks's African-American women is inextricably linked with their sense of race and poverty:
>
>> For Brooks, unlike the Renaissance poets, the victimization of poor Black women becomes not simply a minor chord but a predominant theme of <u>A Street in Bronzeville</u>. Few, if any, of her female characters are able to free themselves from a web of poverty that threatens to strangle their lives. (980)

SAMPLE REFERENCES

The following formats are used for parenthetical references to various kinds of sources used in papers about literature. Keep in mind that the parenthetical reference contains just enough information to enable readers to find the source in the list of works cited at the end of the paper.

An entire work

August Wilson's play <u>Fences</u> treats many themes frequently expressed in modern drama.

When citing an entire work, state the name of the author in your paper instead of in a parenthetical reference.

A work by two or three authors

Myths cut across boundaries and cultural spheres and reappear in strikingly similar forms from country to country (Feldman and Richardson 124).

The effect of a work of literature depends on the audience's predispositions that derive from membership in various social groups (Hovland, Janis, and Kelley 87).

A work by more than three authors

Hawthorne's short stories frequently use a combination of allegorical and symbolic methods (Guerin et al. 91).

The abbreviation *et al.* is Latin for "and others."

A work in an anthology

In his essay "Flat and Round Characters" E. M. Forster distinguishes between one-dimensional characters and those that are well developed (Stevick 223-31).

The parenthetical reference cites the anthology (edited by Stevick) that contains Forster's essay; full information about the anthology appears in the list of works cited.

A work with volume and page numbers

In 1961, one of Albee's plays, <u>The Zoo Story</u>, was
finally performed in America (Eagleton 2:17).

An indirect source

Wagner observed that myth and history stood before
him "with opposing claims" (qtd. in Winkler 10).

The abbreviation *qtd. in* (quoted in) indicates that the quoted material is
not taken from the original source.

A play or poem with numbered lines

"Give thy thoughts no tongue," says Polonius,
"Nor any unproportioned thought his act"
(<u>Ham</u>. 1.3.59-60).

The parentheses contain the act, scene, and line numbers, separated by periods. When included in parenthetical references, titles of the books of the
Bible and well-known literary works are often abbreviated—*Gen.* for *Genesis* and *Ado* for *Much Ado about Nothing*, for example.

"I muse my life-long hate, and without flinch / I
bear it nobly as I live my part," says Claude McKay
in his bitterly ironic poem "The White City" (3-4).

Notice that a slash [/] is used to separate two or three lines of poetry run in
with the text. The parenthetical reference cites the lines quoted. More than
three lines of poetry should be set off like a long prose passage. For special
emphasis, fewer lines may also be set off in this manner. Punctuation,
spelling, and capitalization, and indentation are reproduced *exactly*.

The List of Works Cited

Parenthetical references refer to a **list of works cited** that includes all the
sources you refer to in your paper. (If your list includes all the works consulted, whether you cite them or not, use the title Works Consulted.) Begin
the works cited list on a new page, continuing the page numbers of the pa-

per. For example, if the text of the paper ends on page six, the works cited section will begin on page seven.

Center the title Works Cited one inch from the top of the page. Arrange entries alphabetically, according to the last name of each author (or the first word of the title if the author is unknown). Articles—*a, an,* and *the*—at the beginning of a title are not considered first words. Thus, *A Handbook of Critical Approaches to Literature* would be alphabetized under *H.* In order to conserve space, publishers' names are abbreviated—for example, *Harcourt* for Harcourt Brace College Publishers. Double-space the entire Works Cited list between and within entries. Begin typing each entry at the left margin, and indent subsequent lines five spaces or one-half inch. The entry itself generally has three divisions—author, title, and publishing information—separated by periods. The *MLA Handbook for Writers of Research Papers* (1999) shows a single space after all end punctuation.

A book by a single author

Kingston, Maxine Hong. <u>The Woman Warrior: Memoirs of
    a Girlhood among Ghosts</u>. New York: Knopf, 1976.

A book by two or three authors

Feldman, Burton, and Robert D. Richardson. <u>The Rise
    of Modern Mythology</u>. Bloomington: Indiana UP,
    1972.

Notice that only the *first* author's name is in reverse order.

A book by more than three authors

Guerin, Wilfred, et al., eds. <u>A Handbook of Critical
    Approaches to Literature</u>. 3rd ed. New York:
    Harper, 1992.

Instead of using *et al.,* you may list all the authors' names in the order in which they appear on the title page.

Two or more works by the same author

Novoa, Juan-Bruce. <u>Chicano Authors: Inquiry by In-
    terview</u>, Austin: U of Texas P, 1980.

>   ---. "Themes in Rudolfo Anaya's Work." Address
>   given at New Mexico State University, Las
>   Cruces. 11 Apr. 1987.

List two or more works by the same author in alphabetical order by title. Include the author's full name in the first entry; use three unspaced hyphens followed by a period to take the place of the author's name in second and subsequent entries.

An edited book

>   Oosthuizen, Ann, ed. <u>Sometimes When It Rains: Writ-
>   ings by South African Women</u>. New York: Pandora,
>   1987.

Note that the abbreviation *ed.* stands for *editor.* If there is more than one editor, use *eds.*

A book with a volume number

>   Eagleton, T. Allston. <u>A History of the New York
>   Stage</u>. Vol. 2. Englewood Cliffs: Prentice,
>   1987.

All three volumes have the same title.

>   Durant, Will, and Ariel Durant. <u>The Age of Napoleon:
>   A History of European Civilization from 1789 to
>   1815</u>. New York: Simon, 1975.

Each volume has a different title, so you may cite an individual book without referring to the other volumes.

A short story, poem, or play in a collection of the author's work

>   Gordimer, Nadine. "Once upon a Time." <u>"Jump" and
>   Other Stories</u>. New York: Farrar, 1991. 23–30.

A short story in an anthology

>   Salinas, Marta. "The Scholarship Jacket." <u>Nosotros:
>   Latina Literature Today</u>. Ed. Maria del Carmen

> Boza, Beverly Silva, and Carmen Valle. Binghamton: Bilingual, 1986. 68-70.

The inclusive page numbers follow the year of publication. Note that here the abbreviation *Ed.* stands for *Edited by.*

A poem in an anthology

> Simmerman, Jim. "Child's Grave, Hale County, Alabama." <u>The Pushcart Prize, X: Best of the Small Presses</u>. Ed. Bill Henderson. New York: Penguin, 1986. 198-99.

A play in an anthology

> Hughes, Langston. <u>Mother and Child</u>. <u>Black Drama Anthology</u>. Ed. Woodie King and Ron Miller. New York: NAL, 1986. 399-406.

An article in an anthology

> Forster, E. M. "Flat and Round Characters." <u>The Theory of the Novel</u>. Ed. Philip Stevick. New York: Free, 1980. 223-31.

More than one selection from the same anthology

If you are using more than one selection from an anthology, cite the anthology in one entry. In addition, list each individual selection separately, including the author and title of the selection, the anthology editor's last name, and the inclusive page numbers.

> Kirszner, Laurie G., and Stephen R. Mandell, eds. <u>Literature: Reading, Reacting, Writing</u>. 3rd ed. Fort Worth: Harcourt, 1997.
> Rich, Adrienne. "Diving into the Wreck." Kirszner and Mandell 874-76.

A translation

> Carpentier, Alejo. <u>Reasons of State</u>. Trans. Francis Partridge. New York: Norton, 1976.

An article in a journal with continuous pagination in each issue

    Le Guin, Ursula K. "American Science Fiction and the
        Other." Science Fiction Studies 2 (1975):
        208-10.

An article with separate pagination in each issue

    Grossman, Robert. "The Grotesque in Faulkner's
        'A Rose for Emily.'" Mosaic 20.3 (1987): 40-55.

20.3 signifies volume 20, issue 3.

An article in a magazine

    Milosz, Czeslaw. "A Lecture." New Yorker 22 June
        1992: 32.
    "Solzhenitsyn: An Artist Becomes an Exile." Time
        25 Feb. 1974: 34+.

34+ indicates that the article appears on pages that are not consecutive; in this case the article begins on page 34 and then continues on page 37. An article with no listed author is entered by title on the Works Cited list.

An article in a daily newspaper

    Oates, Joyce Carol. "When Characters from the Page
        Are Made Flesh on the Screen." New York Times
        23 Mar. 1986, late ed.: C1+.

C1+ indicates that the article begins on page 1 of Section C and continues on a subsequent page.

An article in a reference book

    "Dance Theatre of Harlem." The New Encyclopaedia
        Britannica: Micropaedia. 15th ed. 1987.

You do not need to include publication information for well-known reference books.

    Grimstead, David. "Fuller, Margaret Sarah." Encyclo-
        pedia of American Biography. Ed. John A. Gar-
        raty. New York: Harper, 1974.

You must include publication information when citing reference books that are not well known.

A CD-ROM: Entry with a print version

```
Zurbach, Kate. "The Linguistic Roots of Three
     Terms." Linguistic Quarterly 37 (1994): 12-47.
     Infotrac: Magazine Index Plus. CD-ROM. Informa-
     tion Access. Jan. 1996.
```

When you cite information with a print version from a CD-ROM, include the publication information, the underlined title of the database (Infotrac: Magazine Index Plus), the publication medium (CD-ROM), the name of the company that produced the CD-ROM (Information Access), and the electronic publication date.

A CD-ROM: Entry with no print version

```
"Surrealism." Encarta 1996. CD-ROM. Redmond, WA:
     Microsoft, 1996.
```

If you are citing a part of a work, include the title in quotation marks.

```
A Music Lover's Multimedia Guide to Beethoven's 5th.
     CD-ROM. Spring Valley: Interactive, 1993.
```

[If you are citing an entire work, include the underlined title.]

An online source: Entry with a print version

```
Dekoven, Marianne. "Utopias Limited: Post-sixties
     and Postmodern American Fiction." Modern Fic-
     tion Studies 41.1 (1995): 121-34. Online. In-
     ternet. 17 Mar. 1996. <http://muse.jhu.edu/
     journals/MFS/v041/41.1 dekoven.html>.
```

When you cite information with a print version from an online source, include the publication information for the printed source, the number of pages (*n. pag.* if no pages are given), the publication medium (Online), the name of the computer network (Internet), and the date of access. If you wish, you may also include the electronic address. Information from a commercial computer service—America Online, Prodigy, and CompuServ, for example—will not have an electronic address.

O'Hara, Sandra. "Reexamining the Canon." _Time_ 13 May
        1994: 27. Online. America Online. 22 Aug. 1994.

An online source: Entry with no print version

"Romanticism." _Academic American Encyclopedia_. On-
        line. Prodigy. 6 Nov. 1995.

This entry shows that the material was accessed on November 6, 1996.

An online source: Public Posting

Peters, Olaf. "Studying English through German."
        29 Feb. 1996. Online Posting. Foreign Language
        Forum, Multi Language Section. CompuServe.
        15 Mar. 1996.
Gilford, Mary. "Dog Heroes in Children's Litera-
        ture." 4 Oct. 1996. Newsgroup alt.animals.dogs.
        America Online. 23 Mar. 1996.

WARNING: Using information from online forums and newsgroups is
risky. Contributors are not necessarily experts, and frequently they are
incorrect and misinformed. Unless you can be certain that the information you are receiving from these sources is reliable, do not use it in your
papers.

An online source: Electronic Text

Twain, Mark. _Adventures of Huckleberry Finn_. From
        The Writing of Mark Twain. Vol. 13. New York:
        Harper, 1970. Online. Wiretap.spies. Internet.
        13 Jan. 1996. <http.//www.sci.dixie.edu/
        DixieCollege/Ebooks/huckfin.html>.

This electronic text was originally published by Harper. The name of the
repository for the electronic edition is Wiretap.spies.

An online source: E-Mail

Adkins, Camille. E-mail to the author. 8 June 1995.

An interview

> Brooks, Gwendolyn. "Interviews." <u>Triquarterly</u> 60
>   (1984): 405-10.

A lecture or address

> Novoa, Juan-Bruce. "Themes in Rudolfo Anaya's Work."
>   New Mexico State University, Las Cruces,
>   11 Apr. 1987.

A film or videocassette

> "<u>A Worn Path</u>." By Eudora Welty. Dir. John Reid and
>   Claudia Velasco. Perf. Cora Lee Day and Con-
>   chita Ferrell. Videocassette. Harcourt, 1994.

In addition to the title, the director, and the year, include other pertinent information such as the principal performers.

Explanatory Notes

Explanatory notes, indicated by a superscript (a raised number) in the text, may be used to cite several sources at once or to provide commentary or explanations that do not fit smoothly into your paper. The full text of these notes appears on the first numbered page following the last page of the paper. (If your paper has no explanatory notes, the Works Cited page follows the last page of the paper.) Like Works Cited entries, explanatory notes are double-spaced within and between entries. However, the first line of each explanatory note is indented five spaces (or one-half inch), with subsequent lines flush with the left-hand margin.

TO CITE SEVERAL SOURCES

In the paper

> Surprising as it may seem, there have been many
> attempts to define literature.[1]

146 Appendix: Documenting Sources

In the note

¹ For an overview of critical opinion, see Arnold 72; Eagleton 1-2; Howe 43-44; and Abrams 232-34.

To Provide Explanations

In the paper

In recent years Gothic novels have achieved great popularity.³

In the note

³ Gothic novels, works written in imitation of medieval romances, originally relied on supernatural occurrences. They flourished in the late eighteenth and early nineteenth centuries.

Credits

Frederick Asals, "The Aesthetics of Incongruity" from *Flannery O'Connor: The Imagination of Extremity* by Frederick Asals. Reprinted by permission of the University of Georgie Press.

Michael O. Bellamy, "Everything Off Balance: Protestant Election in Flannery O'Connor's 'A Good Man Is Hard to Find'" by Michael O. Bellamy. This essay originally appeared in the *Flannery O'Connor Bulletin* (Vol. 8, 1979, pp. 116–124). Reprinted by permission.

Hallman B. Bryant, "Reading the Map in 'A Good Man Is Hard to Find.'" *Studies in Short Fiction* 18 (1981): 301–07. Copyright 1981 by Newberry College. Reprinted by permission.

Rebecca R. Butler, "What's So Funny About Flannery O'Connor?" by Rebecca R. Butler. This essay originally appeared in the *Flannery O'Connor Bulletin* (Vol. 9, 1980, pp. 30–40). Reprinted by permission.

A. R. Coulthard, "Flannery O'Connor's Deadly Conversions" by A. R. Coulthard. This essay originally appeared in the *Flannery O'Connor Bulletin* (Vol. 13, 1984, pp. 87–98). Reprinted by permission.

Dixie Lee Highsmith, "Flannery O'Connor's Polite Conversation" by Dixie Lee Highsmith. This essay originally appeared in the *Flannery O'Connor Bulletin* (Vol. 11, 1982, pp. 94–107). Reprinted by permission.

Madison Jones, "A Good Man's Predicament" by Madison Jones from *The Southern Review,* Vol. 20, 1984, pp. 836–841. Reprinted by permission of the author.

Flannery O'Connor, "A Good Man Is Hard to Find" from *A Good Man Is Hard to Find,* copyright © 1955 by Flannery O'Connor and renewed 1981 by Regina O'Connor, reprinted by permission of Harcourt Brace & Company. "To a Professor of English: 28 March 61" from *The Habit of Being: Letters by Flannery O'Connor,* edited and selected by Robert Giroux. Copyright © 1979 by Regina O'Connor. Reprinted by permission of Farrar, Straus & Giroux, Inc. Excerpt from "On Her Own Work" from *Mystery and Manners: Occasional Prose* by Flannery O'Connor, edited by Sally Fitzgerald. Copyright © 1969 by the Estate of Mary Flannery O'Connor. Reprinted by permission of Farrar, Straus & Giroux, Inc.